ASTROS STRONG
HOUSTON'S HISTORIC 2017 CHAMPIONSHIP SEASON

SPECIAL COMMEMORATIVE BOOK

This book is book is available in quantity at special discounts for your group or organization. For further information, contact:

Triumph Books LLC
814 North Franklin Street
Chicago, Illinois 60610
Phone: (312) 337-0747
www.triumphbooks.com

Printed in U.S.A.
ISBN: 978-1-62937-486-4

Houston Chronicle
John C. McKeon, Publisher and President
Nancy C. Barnes, Editor and Executive Vice President for News
Vernon Loeb, Managing Editor
Randy Harvey, Sports Editor
Scott Kingsley, Director of Multimedia
Steve Schaeffer, Book Editor/Houston Chronicle Baseball Editor
Laura Goldberg, Senior Editor for New & Niche Products
Reid Laymance, Deputy Sports Editor
Susan Barber, Design Director
Linda A. Schaible, Vice President of Marketing and Audience Development

Content packaged by Mojo Media, Inc.
Joe Funk: Editor
Jason Hinman: Creative Director

Front cover photo by Karen Warren/Houston Chronicle
Back cover photo by Brett Coomer/Houston Chronicle

Mark Mulligan/Houston Chronicle

CONTENTS

INTRODUCTION

By Steve Schaeffer, Houston Chronicle Baseball Editor

Perhaps it was foreshadowed on January 18, when Jeff Bagwell was named an electee to the National Baseball Hall of Fame: 2017 would be the year of the Astros.

Bagwell was elected on his seventh try (or six too many in the eyes of Astros fans), but Houston had grown accustomed to waiting where its baseball team was concerned.

Born as the Colt .45s in 1962, the franchise that in 1965 became the Astros finished 2016 without a championship in 55 years of play. The 2005 team was the only one to have won a pennant but was swept in the World Series by the Chicago White Sox.

The story of the 2017 team really begins in late 2011, when Jim Crane purchased the franchise and hired Jeff Luhnow as its general manager. Jose Altuve had completed his rookie season, and George Springer had been selected in the first round of that year's draft. The silver lining in a 106-loss campaign was that Luhnow would get the first draft pick in 2012, which he used on 17-year-old shortstop Carlos Correa.

Rebuilding yielded two more seasons of triple-digit losses (107 in 2012 and 111 in 2013, their first year as an American League entity), but by the time A.J. Hinch arrived as manager in 2015, the Astros were ready to emerge as a contender. With Correa taking Rookie of the Year honors and Dallas Keuchel registering a Cy Young Award campaign, the Astros won the AL wild card and made the playoffs for the first time in 10 years. They were six outs from advancing to the AL Championship Series before the Kansas City Royals rallied from a four-run deficit in Game 4 and went on to win the AL Division Series in five games.

Unable to overcome a slow start to the 2016 season, the Astros didn't make the playoffs. But in 2017, it all clicked.

Joining Altuve, Springer and Correa in their Core Four was 2016 call-up Alex Bregman, drafted by Luhnow with the second overall selection of 2015. Yuli Gurriel, a star in Cuba, had been procured in 2016. And perhaps as importantly, Luhnow had added a veteran presence to the clubhouse via an offseason trade for Brian McCann and the free-agent signings of Josh Reddick and Carlos Beltran.

A slow start would not be an issue in 2017. The Astros went 16-9 in April, 22-7 in May and 16-11 in June and were 60-29 at the All-Star break, good for a 16.5-game lead atop the AL West. Six Astros – Altuve, Correa, Springer, Keuchel, Lance McCullers Jr. and Chris Devenski – would represent the team at the All-Star Game in Miami.

But it would not be a season without obstacles. At one point, 80 percent of the starting rotation was on the disabled list. Correa and Springer, who at midseason joined Altuve as legitimate MVP candidates, would see DL time in the second half. August would bring the first losing month of the year.

And then there was Harvey.

Starting on the final Saturday of August, with the Astros in California for a series with the Los Angeles Angels, the Houston area was devastated by flooding caused by Hurricane Harvey, with rainfall totaling more than 50 inches over three days in some spots.

Fatalities numbered in the dozens. Those displaced from their homes numbered in the thousands. Did baseball even matter anymore?

Turns out it did. Although the Astros were routed to Tampa to play a three-game "home" series with the Rangers, Houston Mayor Sylvester Turner was insistent that they return to Minute Maid Park for their next scheduled series against the New York Mets. The Astros could offer a welcome diversion, but they went beyond that. On their first full day back, they participated in hurricane relief efforts, immersing themselves in a community in need.

Out of Harvey arose a slogan: Houston Strong. It epitomized a city that would not be defeated by anything inflicted upon it.

And as if on a mission for something beyond themselves, the Astros returned to their winning ways, going 21-8 to close the season and finishing with 101 victories, a total that ranked second in franchise history.

Oh, did we mention Justin Verlander?

On Aug. 31, with seconds to spare in getting the paperwork processed, the Astros acquired the ace righthander in a trade-deadline deal with the Detroit Tigers. The final piece had arrived, confirmed by Verlander's winning all five of his September starts with his new club while posting a 1.06 ERA.

But winning in September is child's play compared to winning in October. A team has to be strong.

Up first in the playoffs were the AL East champion Boston Red Sox in the ALDS. The Astros won the first two games at home, but with Boston in position to even things and force a fifth game, Bregman hit a game-tying homer off Sox ace Chris Sale in the eighth inning, and Josh Reddick delivered the go-ahead single off closer extraordinaire Craig Kimbrel. How strong is that?

Then came the ALCS and the New York Yankees, baseball's most storied franchise, with 27 championships and 40 pennants to its name.

Things were looking good when the Astros tagged another premier closer, Aroldis Chapman, with a ninth-inning run in Game 2 to put them up 2-0 in the series. But the season was on the brink after New York won three consecutive games at Yankee Stadium.

Not to worry. After the series returned to Minute Maid, Verlander won Game 6, and Charlie Morton and McCullers teamed on a 4-0 Game 7 shutout, putting the Astros into the World Series for the second time. Strong stuff.

The final obstacle: the 104-win Los Angeles Dodgers in the first World Series since 1970 to feature a pair of 100-victory clubs.

After best-pitcher-of-his-time Clayton Kershaw mowed down the Astros in Game 1, they won a game for the ages in Game 2. Facing Kenley Jansen, the best closer on earth (and probably the galaxy), Marwin Gonzalez homered to tie the game at 3 in the ninth. Homers by Altuve and Correa put the Astros up 5-3 in the 10th, but the Dodgers evened things in the bottom half. Unfazed, Springer hit a two-run homer in the 11th, and Devenski, despite allowing a solo homer, held on for the biggest save of his career to seal the 7-6 victory.

A split of Games 3 and 4 left things tied. Cue another game for the ages.

In Game 5, the Astros overcame 4-1, 7-4 and 8-7 deficits – scoring six runs off Kershaw in the process – and held a 12-9 lead after eight innings. Then a three-run L.A. ninth elevated this one to an epic that will be hard to match. The minute-by-Minute Maid drama would end an inning later, when Bregman's RBI single off Jansen gave the Astros a 13-12 decision in the greatest game Houston's downtown ballpark has seen.

With a shift back to L.A., the Series was pushed to its max when the Dodgers beat Verlander in a 3-1 Game 6. But with Springer tying a Series record with his fifth home run as the Astros took a 5-0 lead in the second inning of Game 7, five pitchers teamed to shut down the Dodgers 5-1. Morton sparkled over the final four innings, and when Gurriel gloved Altuve's throw from second to first for the final out, there was rejoicing in H-town.

In what had been a heavyweight prize fight in baseball form, the Astros emerged strongest.

Now comes the savoring. The highlights of the most memorable season in Astros annals, as reported and photographed by the supremely talented staff members who covered the team for the Houston Chronicle, are contained within these pages.

It was a year that will reverberate in Houston for decades to come. Finally, for the first time in their history, the Astros wore the crown of world champions.

They galvanized a city. And a city galvanized them.

They were Houston Strong. They were Astros Strong. ■

Game 1
October 24, 2017 • Los Angeles, California
Dodgers 3, Astros 1

KERPLUNK

Kershaw Throws 11-K Game for Dodgers; Keuchel Takes Fall

By Jake Kaplan

The major league-best offense on which the Astros' 101-win season was built thrived not only because of its power but because of its ability to make contact. Their lineup proved the most difficult to strike out while also leading baseball in slugging percentage.

But none of that seemed to matter with Clayton Kershaw on the mound Tuesday night for the first World Series game at Dodger Stadium since 1988. The lefthander is the greatest pitcher of his generation, and in the biggest start yet in his Hall of Fame-worthy career, he made the Astros his victims.

The Astros managed to put only three runners on base in Game 1 of the Fall Classic, resulting in a 3-1 loss that renders Wednesday night's Game 2 all but a must win for the American League champions. They struck out 12 times, a total they reached or eclipsed only four times during the regular season. The hitting-with-runners-in-scoring-position column didn't even make the visitors' side of the box score.

Kershaw, a former MVP and a three-time Cy Young Award winner, became the first pitcher to strike out 11 in a World Series game since Arizona's Randy Johnson in Game 2 in 2001. Before Kershaw on Tuesday, Don Newcombe had been the only pitcher to record 11 strikeouts without issuing a walk in a World Series game. He accomplished the feat for the Brooklyn Dodgers in 1949.

"Sometimes you have to tip the hat to the other team," Astros second baseman Jose Altuve said. "I think that's the case today."

Dodgers manager Dave Roberts rode Kershaw for only seven innings and 83 pitches before turning over the game to shutdown relievers Brandon Morrow and Kenley Jansen. The Astros received a winnable start from Dallas Keuchel, who pitched 6 2/3 innings but was doomed by his offense's failure to hit Los Angeles' pitching.

Dodgers postseason hero Justin Turner was responsible for the biggest swing of the game, which was played in a brisk two hour, 28 minutes, the shortest for a World Series game in a quarter century. The stadium, which hosted 54,253 mostly blue-and-white clad fans, shook after Turner's two-run homer in the sixth inning broke a tie.

"I didn't know if it was going to be a home run or not," Turner said. "I knew I backspun it pretty good. I knew I hit it really high. And I knew it was about 98 degrees. So when it's that hot here, the ball does travel a lot better. … If it's 10 degrees cooler, that's probably a routine fly ball in left field."

The 103-degree weather at first pitch made for the hottest World Series game in recorded history. In a performance reminiscent of the first five games of their AL Championship Series against the Yankees, the Astros' bats went cold.

"I don't think it has anything to do with the ALCS. That's a completely different pitching staff," Astros manager A.J. Hinch said. "Tonight is about Kershaw."

Kershaw, a 10-year veteran who's only 29, became the first pitcher all season to strike out 11 Astros in a start. Only two – Cleveland's Corey Kluber and Philadelphia's Aaron Nola – reached double digits against them during the regular season.

The Astros, who fell to 0-5 all-time in World Series games, will have to hit lefthander Rich Hill on Wednesday to muster a split before the series moves to Houston.

"This team is a really good hitting team. They hit a lot of homers and don't strike out. There's little room for error," Kershaw said. "So it's important for me to establish pitches, be able to throw multiple things for strikes, and thankfully, I was able to do that tonight."

A solo home run by Alex Bregman and singles by Altuve and Josh Reddick signified the Astros' output.

Jose Altuve flies out to end Game 1 of the World Series. Altuve had one of only three hits for the Astros on the night. (Michael Ciaglo/Houston Chronicle)

George Springer went 0-for-4 with four strikeouts. Carlos Correa, Yuli Gurriel, Brian McCann and Marwin Gonzalez were each 0-for-3. Two of Kershaw's strikeouts came against Keuchel.

"(Kershaw) just did a great job of commanding the plate tonight," said Springer, who is without an extra-base hit since the Division Series. "He was able to throw his slider with depth. He was able to throw it across, in, and then spot up his heater. He threw the ball well. There's really nothing else to say about it."

Keuchel also pitched well but surrendered two costly homers. Chris Taylor, who shared NLCS MVP honors with Turner, got the 113th Fall Classic started by launching Keuchel's first pitch of the game 447 feet to left field. The blast was the fourth leadoff home run in the history of World Series Game 1s. Taylor ambushed an 87 mph fastball thrown down and inside.

Keuchel regrouped immediately. The ground-ball inducer extraordinaire faced only one batter more than the minimum through five innings. He was backed by three double plays turned behind him.

In the sixth, Keuchel extracted consecutive groundouts to Correa at shortstop. But in his third battle with Taylor, he issued the game's first walk. Against

Turner, he jumped ahead to a 1-and-2 count. After he had beaten the Dodgers third baseman on cutters in his two previous at-bats, Keuchel decided to go back to the pitch, this one high and inside. Turner, who had switched to a smaller bat, got to it.

"That one was a tough one to swallow," Keuchel said.

All of the game's runs scored via long balls. In the fourth inning, Bregman made Kershaw pay for a 1-and-1 fastball he left over the middle by lining it over the left-field fence. At 23, Bregman became the youngest AL player to homer in the World Series since a 23-year-old Manny Ramirez took Atlanta's Mark Wohlers deep in Game 4 of the 1995 series between the Indians and Braves.

But other than Bregman, the Astros couldn't touch Kershaw. The Dallas native thrived behind a fastball that sat at 93 mph, a slider he ran up to 90 mph, and a curveball in the mid-70s. The performance marked the fifth time in 18 career postseason starts he reached double digits in strikeouts. It was his third career postseason start in which he didn't issue a walk.

"He's a great pitcher. He's going to the Hall of Fame," Bregman said. "He pitched really well. He made some good pitches. He made some good marginal pitches on the way. It's all right. We'll show up ready to go (in Game 2)." ▪

Game 2
October 25, 2017 • Los Angeles, California
Astros 7, Dodgers 6 (11 innings)

HOMER HAPPY

Springer's Decisive Blow in 11th Follows Blasts by Gonzalez, Altuve, Correa
By Jake Kaplan

George Springer etched his name in Astros lore with the biggest hit in franchise history Wednesday night at Dodger Stadium.

Springer drove a go-ahead two-run homer to right-center field in the top of the 11th inning to propel the Astros to their first win in a World Series game in 56 seasons of franchise history. The American League champions mashed four home runs from the ninth inning on to fuel a 7-6 victory over the Los Angeles Dodgers and even the Fall Classic at 1-1.

After a day of rest and travel, Game 3 brings the action back home to Minute Maid Park. It will have a difficult time living up to the bedlam that ensued in Game 2.

"(It was) probably as nerve-wracking as it is in the stands for everybody else," Springer said. "You know who's on the other team, you know who's on deck, and you know who's hitting. And when that last out is made, you finally breathe."

Before Springer's heroics, Marwin Gonzalez, Jose Altuve and Carlos Correa each took turns playing hero.

With the Astros just three outs from a 2-0 series deficit, Gonzalez belted a game-tying solo shot in the ninth against the usually unhittable Dodgers closer Kenley Jansen. In a 10th that at the time appeared to shift the momentum for good, Altuve and Correa homered in back-to-back at-bats against ex-Astro Josh Fields to open a two-run lead.

Correa punctuated his homer with an epic bat flip and channeled his inner Yasiel Puig when asked about it after the game.

"Like one friend of mine once said," Correa said, "I don't know why my bats are so slippery."

But after Altuve and Correa put the game back in the Astros' hands in the top of the 10th, Ken Giles blew the lead in the bottom of the frame. On the heels of a perfect ninth, Giles began the 10th by surrendering a home run to Puig. A two-out walk to Logan Forsythe, a wild pitch and a single by Kiké Hernandez tied the game.

Springer, who with Cameron Maybin on second base cranked a 2-and-1 slider from Dodgers righthander Brandon McCarthy, bailed out the Astros closer. Chris Devenski recorded the final four outs but not before allowing a solo homer to Charlie Culberson with two outs in the 11th, the eighth home run of the game, which set a World Series record.

"I just need to go out there and execute better," said Giles, who has allowed a run or more in five of his six postseason outings. "I've just got to do a better job flat out."

The Astros were 0-5 all-time in World Series games before Wednesday's dramatic comeback. Altuve and Correa became the first teammates in World Series history to hit extra-inning homers in the same game, let alone doing it back-to-back. Gonzalez became the first visiting player to tie a World Series game with a ninth-inning homer since the Red Sox's Dwight Evans in Game 3 of the 1975 Series against the Reds.

Marwin Gonzalez hits a home run during the ninth inning of Game 2, tying the game at 3-3 and forcing extra innings. (Michael Ciaglo/Houston Chronicle)

Altuve, Correa and Springer also made the Astros the first team to hit three homers in extra innings of a postseason game.

"That's got to be one of the best games ever," Astros third baseman Alex Bregman said. "Just both teams battling it out. And the 'Stros finished on top."

Springer went 3-for-5 in the game. The All-Star center fielder doubled off Jansen in the ninth, his first extra-base hit since the ALDS. He had gone 0-for-4 with four strikeouts in Game 1 of the Series. He came into Game 2 with only three hits in his previous 30 at-bats.

"I just think when the lights turn on even brighter, you tend to subconsciously press, and you want to succeed so bad that you start to do things that you wouldn't do, or you start to come out of an approach that has worked the whole year," he said.

"And this is my first experience at playing this far, playing this long, and in a game of this magnitude. So for me to kind of experience it and to kind of understand, 'Hey, slow yourself down,' I understand now why guys struggle in the postseason and some don't."

Said Correa, grinning: "He's back, man. He gets really scary when he's back."

The Astros improved to 10-0 in games in which Justin Verlander has pitched since they acquired the former MVP and Cy Young Award winner from the Detroit Tigers on Aug. 31. Verlander exited with a two-run deficit despite giving up only two hits. Both left the yard.

So did four long balls off the Astros' bats. Making Gonzalez's ninth-inning blast more impressive was the count in which he hit it. He fell behind 0-2 against Jansen before getting a 94 mph cutter over the plate.

"I told Marwin the inning before, I told him he was going to win the ballgame for us," Verlander said. "I didn't think it was going to be a game-tying home run. I thought it was going to be game-winning. That's what I told him."

The Astros outhit the Dodgers 14-5. Six of their runs came against a Dodgers bullpen that saw its streak of 28 consecutive scoreless innings snapped. The Astros contended with curveballing lefthander Rich Hill for only 60 pitches before Dodgers manager Dave Roberts turned to his vaunted bullpen. Hill went through the Astros' lineup two times and allowed a run on three singles and a walk against seven strikeouts.

Bregman opened the scoring with a single to center field that plated Josh Reddick in the third inning, the Astros' first run before the fourth inning of a game since the ALDS.

For the rest of the game, the Astros faced an ensemble of relief pitchers. Kenta Maeda gave the Dodgers four outs before lefthanded specialist Tony Watson recorded two outs with one pitch, which he used to extract a double-play grounder from Brian McCann to end the top of the sixth. Ross Stripling and Brandon Morrow served as the rest of the bridge to Jansen.

Verlander completed six innings before Astros manager A.J. Hinch pinch-hit for him. In another weird twist, Verlander's outing featured an eerily similar game-changing sequence to the one Dallas Keuchel experienced in the Astros' Game 1 loss.

A night after Justin Turner tagged Keuchel for a two-run homer in the sixth, Corey Seager flipped the game with a two-run homer in the sixth. Both were hit with two outs and in pitcher-friendly 1-and-2 counts. Both were hit after Chris Taylor grinded out a two-out walk. Both exited the field of play in left.

Relievers Will Harris and Joe Musgrove kept the game close for the Astros with scoreless innings in the seventh and eighth, respectively. Giles followed with a perfect ninth.

Then ... madness.

"That's an incredible game on so many levels, so many ranges of emotion," Hinch said. "If you like October baseball, if you like any kind of baseball, that's one of the most incredible games you'll ever be a part of." ∎

George Springer celebrates his two-run home run in the 11th inning of Game 2. Springer's homer proved to be the decisive blow as the Astros won 7-6 in 11 innings. (Karen Warren/Houston Chronicle)

Game 3
October 27, 2017 • Houston, Texas
Astros 5, Dodgers 3

SAVORY SAVE

Peacock Records Last 11 Outs, Preserves Victory for McCullers
By Jake Kaplan

Fifty minutes after right fielder Josh Reddick gloved the final out of a victory Friday night that left the Astros two more shy of their first World Series title, Brad Peacock was still in disbelief. Peacock had just converted a 3 2/3-inning save to cap a 5-3 win over the Los Angeles Dodgers in Game 3 of the World Series. He did for Lance McCullers Jr. what McCullers did for Charlie Morton in Game 7 of the American League Championship Series. He shut down the game.

"I can't believe what just happened out there," Peacock said on his way out of the Astros' clubhouse at Minute Maid Park just before midnight.

His save, the first of a career that dates to 2011, marked the longest relief outing in the World Series since San Francisco star Madison Bumgarner pitched five legendary innings to close out the 2014 Fall Classic. But this was Brad Peacock, an unassuming 29-year-old righthander so unsure of his status with the Astros that before spring training he warned his wife they might have to move to Japan.

Against the Dodgers on the biggest stage baseball offers, Peacock retired 11 of the 12 batters he faced. He didn't allow a hit on his way to closing the Astros' first win in a World Series game played in Houston, a win that put them ahead in the series two games to one.

A four-run barrage against Dodgers starter Yu Darvish stood as the Astros' primary source of offense. They chased Darvish, the ex-Texas Rangers ace, in

their big second inning. McCullers, while far from his sharpest, gave the Astros a solid 5 1/3 innings before Astros manager A.J. Hinch let Peacock fly for the rest of the game.

"This postseason, I've really enjoyed bringing back the three-inning save," Hinch quipped. "That's cool."

The Astros pummeled Darvish, who had been dominant in his previous postseason starts against the Arizona Diamondbacks and Chicago Cubs. On Friday, his pitches looked flat. Of the 49 pitches the Japanese righthander threw, only one extracted a swing and miss. Many more were scorched or fouled off.

Darvish lasted only 1 2/3 innings, the first time in 136 starts since he debuted in the majors he didn't complete at least three. It was his first time not registering even one strikeout. He issued only one walk but six hits, four that went for extra bases.

"He just left some balls up over the plate today," said Astros center fielder George Springer, who led off the game with a double. "He lives on getting you to chase his stuff. For us today to come out and capitalize on some mistakes was big."

Yuli Gurriel sparked the Astros' four-run second inning with a home run into the Crawford Boxes that registered an exit velocity of 104.3 mph. Jose Altuve cranked a double at 107.5 mph. Even an out by Springer came off his bat at 104.9 mph, a sacrifice fly by Alex Bregman off his at 103.5.

By the time Dodgers manager Dave Roberts replaced

Brad Peacock was an unlikely hero in Game 3, going 3 2/3 innings for the first save of his career. (Karen Warren/Houston Chronicle)

Darvish with Kenta Maeda, the Astros led 4-0.

"The fastball command wasn't there, and the slider was backing up," Roberts said. "So he just really didn't have the feel and couldn't get any type of rhythm going. So right there, you find yourself after five outs down 4-0, you have to go right there – had to go to the pen to give us a chance to stay in that game."

Roberts used five different relievers to get through the night. Maeda gave Los Angeles 2 2/3 dominant innings, which also probably will render him unavailable until at least Sunday.

McCullers overcame an off night to record 16 outs for the Astros. After his offense exploded for four runs in the second, the shutdown third inning eluded him. McCullers lost command of his fastball and his curveball, which resulted in walks to the eight- and nine-hole hitters, Joc Pederson and Kiké Hernandez, and leadoff man Chris Taylor to begin the frame.

But just after Hinch called for Peacock to begin warming up, McCullers induced a ground ball from Corey Seager. Gurriel fielded it by first base and fired to second, where shortstop Carlos Correa received it and fired back to first to a covering McCullers for the double play. A run scored to make it 4-1, but the double play limited the damage significantly, which is what Correa reminded the pitcher on his way back to the mound.

"The best outcome right here is one run in this inning, so go out there and get this guy," Correa told McCullers, who then induced an inning-ending groundout from Justin Turner.

After the Astros took advantage of a throwing error by L.A. lefthander Tony Watson to tack on an insurance run in the fifth, the Dodgers got the run back and one more in the sixth. McCullers issued a leadoff walk to Seager before spinning a two-strike curveball that Turner ripped down the third-base line for a double.

After McCullers struck out Cody Bellinger for a third time, Hinch pulled him in favor of Peacock to face Yasiel Puig. A groundout narrowed the Astros' lead to three runs. A wild pitch by Peacock on a slider to pinch hitter Chase Utley plated Turner and made it a 5-3 game.

For the remainder of the night, Peacock showed very little of his slider, the pitch that revitalized his career. Catcher Brian McCann kept calling for the fastball, and the pitcher who rarely if ever shakes his catchers obliged.

During a brief visit in the ninth inning amid his final battle against Yasmani Grandal, Peacock asked McCann how he felt about trying a changeup. "Absolutely not," McCann replied.

"It was exploding on them," McCann said of Peacock's fastball, which averaged 94 mph Friday. "(I was) just seeing funny swings and funny takes . He's got one of the better fastballs in the game, too. He's got one of those, like, balls that rides on the same plane. He's got a two-seamer and a four-seamer, so it's kind of two different pitches in one. The hitters tell you a lot from their reactions, and we just kept going with it."

Peacock, who started for the Astros in the Division Series before he was replaced in the rotation by McCullers in the ALCS, threw 53 pitches to get the final 11 outs. His was the third-longest relief outing in Astros postseason history after McCullers' four-inning save in Game 7 of the ALCS and Collin McHugh's four scoreless innings in Game 3 of the ALCS.

"Honestly, I've expected what he's done this year every year since he's been here," said ace lefthander Dallas Keuchel, a teammate since Peacock joined the Astros in 2013. "I've told him that myself. You can ask him. I've always had high hopes for him. He's got some of the best stuff on the team, if not the best stuff overall.

"That's why they've kept him. He's had a few injuries, a few setbacks. So when you really look at it, he hadn't gotten much repetition in the big leagues, and he's had some decent success. So what he finally did was he had a healthy year and just kind of built on each outing. ... He's just that guy who wants to do anything to help the team."

For Peacock, a former 41st-round draft pick of the Washington Nationals who was for years plagued by a balky back, Friday night was hard to fathom. "Wow," he said quietly before accompanying McCullers to a press conference.

"I don't think anybody called that in spring training," Peacock joked later.

When he finally exited the Astros' clubhouse at 11:57 p.m., a man in Astros garb who happened to be walking by stuck out his fist for a pound and said, "Peacock, that was (bleeping) beautiful, baby." Meanwhile, loud chants of "Let's Go Peacock" emanated from down the hall, where his parents, sisters and wife and four close friends from back home in West Palm Beach, Fla., awaited him.

"It's crazy," Peacock said. "A crazy year for me." ∎

Yuli Gurriel blasts a solo home run off Yu Darvish, one of four runs allowed by the Dodgers starter.
(Brett Coomer/Houston Chronicle)

Game 4
October 28, 2017 • Houston, Texas
Dodgers 6, Astros 2

NIGHTMARE NINTH

Giles, Musgrove Hammered in Five-Run Inning as L.A. Evens Series

By Jake Kaplan

Ken Giles' miserable postseason continues.

Giles, who has allowed a run or more in six of seven outings in these playoffs, surrendered the runs that doomed the Astros in a 6-2 loss to the Los Angeles Dodgers in Game 4 of the World Series on Saturday night at Minute Maid Park.

The defeat evened the series at two games apiece, ensuring the Fall Classic will return to Los Angeles for at least Game 6. Dodgers lefthander Clayton Kershaw, the best pitcher of his generation, looms in Game 5 on Sunday night. The Astros will counter with Dallas Keuchel in a rematch of Game 1.

"I didn't do my job. Plain and simple," Giles said. "I let the team down."

Summoned to face the heart of the Dodgers' order in the top of the ninth of a 1-1 game, Giles faced only three batters. Each reached base. The maligned Astros closer walked off the mound to boos after allowing a run-scoring double to Cody Bellinger.

Giles' eight pitches Saturday would seem to be the last he will throw in high-leverage situations in this World Series. But only time will tell.

"They were all crappy pitches. Not where I want them," Giles said. "I need to do better. I need to carry my weight. I need to do better for these guys."

The Astros, who scored on an Alex Bregman homer in the bottom of the ninth off Dodgers closer Kenley Jansen, managed only two hits in the game. Both left the yard. They weren't enough.

Giles was charged with three runs and didn't record an out. He gave up a single to Corey Seager and walked Justin Turner before Bellinger struck with his double. Two of the runs charged to Giles scored with Joe Musgrove on the mound. Musgrove was responsible for two runs of his own when he served up a game-breaking three-run homer to Joc Pederson with two outs in the inning.

"The Pederson pitch was right where I wanted, a fastball up out of the zone, and he just beat me to it," Musgrove said. "That's baseball. You get away with plenty of fastballs right down the middle that guys foul off or swing through, and you throw one up out of the zone where you want, and they beat you on it. That's just baseball."

The bullpen meltdown and offensive futility wasted a stellar start. Charlie Morton, a hero in the Astros' Game 7 win in the AL Championship Series, gave his team another dominant outing. In 6 1/3 innings, he allowed only three baserunners. He struck out seven without issuing a walk. Only after he exited was he charged with a run.

Will Harris was on the mound when Logan Forsythe lined a game-tying single to center field with two outs in the seventh. Moments earlier, after allowing a one-out double to Bellinger, Morton had walked off to a standing ovation, which he acknowledged with a tip of his cap. But once Bellinger scored, Morton was ensured a no-decision.

Ken Giles gave up three earned runs and picked up the loss, continuing a rough postseason for the closer. (Brett Coomer/Houston Chronicle)

"I think (catcher Brian McCann) did a good job. We're on the same page, and we had a good game plan going in," Morton said. "I thought we did a pretty good job with the righties, working them in, getting the sinker in on their hands. The curveball was doing all right. I made some good pitches and got some plays behind me.

"But yeah, I wish we could've pulled it out."

George Springer broke up lefthander Alex Wood's no-hitter via a solo homer into the Crawford Boxes with two outs in the sixth inning. The 3-and-1 knuckle curveball Springer punished was Wood's 84th pitch of the night. It was also his last. After Springer rounded the bases, Dodgers manager Dave Roberts emerged to pull his starter.

Wood's command didn't look as sharp his first time through the Astros' lineup as his line would suggest. Springer's sixth-inning at-bat represented the first batter of Wood's third time through the lineup. If Wood had yielded a hit earlier in his outing, it is unlikely Roberts would have allowed his starter to face Springer a third time.

But with a no-hitter intact, Roberts managed to it. The Astros capitalized, with Springer playing hero for the second time in a three-game span.

Roberts extracted from Brandon Morrow and Tony Watson a combined seven outs to bridge the gap to Jansen, who was still deployed for the bottom of the ninth after the Dodgers opened up a five-run lead. Jansen gave up a two-out homer to Alex Bregman before getting a game-ending fly out from Jose Altuve.

Both teams struggled offensively from the start. After Chris Taylor led off the game with a single up the middle against Morton, neither team managed a hit until L.A.'s Kiké Hernandez sliced a single to center field in the sixth.

Between the first-inning single by Taylor and an errant 0-and-1 fastball that hit Barnes in the right forearm to begin the sixth, Morton retired 14 consecutive batters. Barnes advanced to third on Hernandez's single, which he hit on a full-count fastball.

The first-and-third jam with one out represented either team's first offensive threat, especially considering that the Dodgers had the top of their order rolling around. But Morton induced a ground ball to third baseman Bregman, who cut down Barnes at home. A fly out by Seager stranded runners on first and second.

As he was in Game 7 of the ALCS seven nights

earlier, Morton was efficient Saturday. He threw only 76 pitches to record his 19 outs. Harris was left in only for the final two outs of the seventh. Astros manager A.J. Hinch tabbed Chris Devenski for the eighth.

Devenski needed only 12 pitches to complete a perfect inning. He froze Pederson on a 2-and-2 changeup high in the zone, then induced a fly out from Hernandez and a groundout from Taylor. But despite his excellence, Devenski was not afforded another inning. In the middle of the eighth, Giles began to warm in the Astros' bullpen.

Disaster loomed. ■

Gurriel Suspended for Racially Insensitive Gesture

Major League Baseball commissioner Rob Manfred announced Saturday a five-game suspension for Astros first baseman Yuli Gurriel as a result of the racially insensitive gesture Gurriel made during Game 3 of the World Series on Friday night at Minute Maid Park.

The suspension will be effective at the start of the 2018 regular season, which will allow Gurriel to play in the rest of the World Series. Gurriel will not be paid his salary during his suspension, the sum of which the Astros said they will donate to charity. MLB said Gurriel must undergo sensitivity training in the offseason.

Gurriel, 33, made the gesture, caught by television cameras, after hitting a home run off Dodgers starter Yu Darvish in the second inning of the Astros' Game 3 win. After taking a seat on the dugout bench, Gurriel used his fingers to act as if he was slanting his eyes and also appeared to say the Spanish word "Chinito," which translates to "little Chinese boy." Darvish is from Japan.

At a pregame news conference, Manfred laid out his reasoning for delaying Gurriel's suspension until next season as opposed to having him serve a suspension immediately.

"First of all, I felt it was important that the suspension carried with it the penalty of lost salary," Manfred said. "Secondly, I felt it was unfair to punish the other 24 players on the Astros' roster. I wanted the burden of this discipline to fall primarily on the wrongdoer.

"Third, I was impressed in my conversation with Yu Darvish by his desire to move forward, and I felt that moving this suspension to the beginning of the season

Brian McCann chases Dodgers catcher Austin Barnes during Game 4 of the World Series. McCann continued his quiet postseason with no hits and two strikeouts. (Brett Coomer/Houston Chronicle)

would help in that regard. Last, when I originally began thinking about the discipline, I thought that delaying the suspension would allow the player the opportunity to exercise his rights under the grievance procedure."

Gurriel will not appeal the suspension. The Cuban started at first base and batted fifth for the Astros in Game 4 on Saturday night. Manfred met with Gurriel before Saturday's game. Gurriel expressed remorse, according to Manfred, and assured the commissioner he will offer a private apology to Darvish.

"During last night's game, I made an offensive gesture that was indefensible," Gurriel said in a prepared statement released by the Astros. "I sincerely apologize to everyone that I offended with my actions. I deeply regret it. I would particularly like to apologize to Yu Darvish, a pitcher that I admire and respect. I would also like to apologize to the Dodgers organization, the Astros, Major League Baseball and to all fans across the game." ■

Game 5
October 29, 2017 • Houston, Texas
Astros 13, Dodgers 12 (10 innings)

RELENTLESS

Bregman Ends Back-and-Forth Classic with 10th-Inning Single off Jansen
By Jake Kaplan

The epic Game 2 of this World Series has nothing on the all-timer that was Game 5.

In a back-and-forth battle between two heavyweights, the Astros overcame three deficits and countless momentum swings to defeat the Los Angeles Dodgers 13-12 in 10 innings on Sunday night. The final Minute Maid Park crowd of the season was treated to a game that was all sorts of crazy and ultimately left the American League champions one win away from their first championship.

Game 6 is Tuesday night at Dodger Stadium. It will be nearly impossible for it to top its predecessor. In a five-hour, 17-minute marathon that required a 10th inning before Alex Bregman delivered a walk off single against Kenley Jansen, the Astros slugged five home runs, three of which tied the game, and the Dodgers hit two, one that put them ahead.

Fourteen pitchers combined to throw 417 pitches. Neither ace, the Astros' Dallas Keuchel or the Dodgers' Clayton Kershaw, completed even five innings. Four of the top five batters in the Astros' lineup homered. The mess that is the Astros' bullpen led manager A.J. Hinch to deploy Brad Peacock for 39 pitches after he threw 53 two nights earlier.

No lead was safe, not even after the Astros' four-run barrage in the seventh inning off Dodgers reliever Brandon Morrow. Or after Brian McCann tagged Tony Cingrani for a solo home run in the eighth to put the Astros ahead 12-9.

The thriller marked only the second game in World Series history in which both teams scored 12 runs or more, joining Game 4 of the 1993 Fall Classic, a 15-14 Toronto win over Philadelphia. The home runs brought the series total to 22, already a record for a World Series.

As far as longest World Series games go, Sunday's ranks second to only the 14-inning Game 3 of the 2005 series between the Astros and White Sox, also played at Minute Maid Park.

"When you feel like you came through for your team and you see the joy on their faces, there's nothing like it," Bregman said. "It's such a special feeling that I'm so fortunate and blessed to feel today. It's an unbelievable moment. You dream about it as a little kid. To be living a dream, one win away from the World Series, is really special."

Bregman and the Astros finished the instant-classic Game 5 with a two-out rally against the best closer in baseball. It began when Jansen hit McCann on the right wrist with a two-strike cutter. George Springer followed by drawing a walk, at which point Hinch pinch-ran Derek Fisher for the slow-footed McCann at second base.

Bregman didn't waste any time in playing hero. He offered at a first-pitch cutter and sent it to left field, scoring the speedy Fisher. The home dugout emptied before Fisher had even crossed home plate.

"That guy is something, man," Springer said of Bregman. "He lives for stuff like this. He loves it. I watched

Alex Bregman hits a walk off single to score pinch runner Derek Fisher to give the Astros a thrilling 13-12 win over the Dodgers. (Karen Warren/Houston Chronicle)

him dig in the box that last at-bat a little bit harder. You could just see it in his body that he wanted this game to end and he was going to be the guy to do it."

The offense produced in the game was almost too much too track. Jose Altuve, responsible for the second of the Astros' three game-tying home runs, drove in four runs. Carlos Correa and Yuli Gurriel each drove in three, the latter on a blast off Kershaw that tied the game in the fourth inning.

Kershaw, the greatest pitcher on the planet, blew a 4-0 lead for the Dodgers. That alone would have been unpredictable enough to make for an epic game. By the time the final out was recorded, it was a distant memory.

It was fitting the Astros' Core Four players fueled the decisive four-run seventh. Springer sparked the barrage when he crushed a first-pitch fastball from Morrow over the train tracks to tie the game at 8.

Bregman ensured the rally didn't stop there. He, too, offered at the first pitch, a slider, and laced a single to center field. Altuve drove in the go-ahead run with a double to left-center field. Correa followed with a towering fly ball that hung in the air for seemingly forever before landing in one of the first couple rows of the Crawford Boxes.

Correa's two-run homer, which traveled only an estimated 328 feet, put the Astros ahead 11-8. Morrow, who has pitched in every game of the series, threw only six pitches. He allowed four runs.

After McCann's homer off Cingrani in the ninth put the Astros ahead 12-9, Chris Devenski failed to hold the lead. He issued a leadoff walk to Cody Bellinger before serving up a two-run homer to Yasiel Puig. An Austin Barnes double put the tying run in scoring position. With two outs, Chris Taylor plated him on a single up the middle.

Joe Musgrove pitched a scoreless 10th to set the stage for the Astros' rally. The 24-year-old righthander would have pitched the 11th, too. Of the eight members of the Astros' bullpen, only the beleaguered Ken Giles and Francisco Liriano didn't pitch in Game 5.

"Dude, I can't tell you how many times I've said this is the craziest game of my life," Musgrove said. "I mean, again tonight, this is the craziest game of my life."

The Dodgers went ahead 8-7 in the top of the

seventh on a line drive off the bat of Bellinger. Springer, the Astros' All-Star center fielder, charged inward as Kiké Hernandez hedged between first and second base.

Springer miscalculated. Rather than playing for the single and holding Bellinger to the single, he dived. The ball bounced in front of his glove and hopped over it and toward the wall. Hernandez scored easily to give Los Angeles a one-run lead. Bellinger stopped at third.

The sequence came moments after the Astros cut down a potential Dodgers threat. Peacock, deployed despite logging 3 2/3 innings two nights earlier, cut down Justin Turner at third base on a poor sacrifice bunt attempt by Hernandez. Turner reached second on a leadoff double that fell mere inches shy of clearing the fence in right-center field.

In the bottom half of the frame, Springer redeemed himself.

"That's about as low to about as high as you could probably feel at the time," he said. "I made a bad decision. I tried to make a play, but ultimately, I should've stopped. But then to come out and to tie it, that's a feeling that I don't think I can ever describe to anybody."

Although they made for a pitchers' duel in Game 1, neither Keuchel nor Kershaw held up his end of the bargain in Game 5.

Keuchel completed only 3 2/3 innings and allowed three earned runs. Kershaw finished just 4 2/3 and was charged with six earned runs.

Both watched most of the game from the dugout.

"Honestly, it felt like I didn't even pitch," Keuchel said. "And, I mean, I didn't pitch that long. I've never been so nervous in my life. The bubble gut feeling, the highs, the lows. I'm glad that us pitchers are with the No. 1 offense and they provided a good show."

The game began in just about the worst fashion possible for the Astros. Nothing went right. Keuchel allowed a leadoff single to Taylor and issued back-to-back walks to Turner and Hernandez. He hung a two-out slider to Logan Forsythe that scored Taylor easily. Marwin Gonzalez booted a ball in left to ensure Turner also scored.

With Puig at the plate, Keuchel picked off Forsythe, his teammate at the University of Arkansas. As Forsythe ran to second base, Gurriel made a high throw from first base that pulled Altuve off the second-base bag.

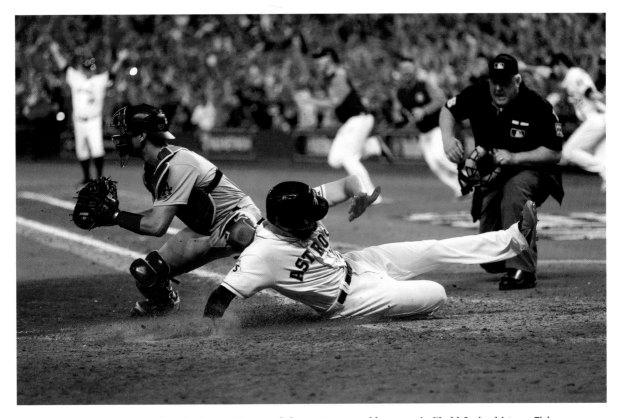

Derek Fisher slides home for the winning run in one of the most memorable games in World Series history. Fisher came on as a pinch runner for Brian McCann, who was hit by a pitch to start the rally. (Brett Coomer/Houston Chronicle)

Hernandez took off for home. In a close play at the base, Forsythe was safe. The Dodgers led 3-0 before Kershaw even took the mound.

The Astros' deficit reached four when Barnes smacked a run-scoring single off Keuchel with two outs in the fourth. In the first of many stunning twists, it proved fleeting.

Kershaw, who had faced the minimum through three, folded in the fourth. Springer led off with a walk. Altuve singled. Correa whacked a run-scoring double. Then came the big blow. The always-aggressive Gurriel capitalized on a first-pitch hanging slider and tied the game with a three-run shot to left field.

Collin McHugh came on at the start of the fifth for his first appearance since Game 3 of the AL Championship Series. It didn't take more than a few pitches to see he didn't have it. McHugh walked Seager and Turner before giving up a three-run homer to Bellinger.

The bottom of the fifth proved just as nutty, though.

With two outs and the bases empty, Springer drew a walk against Kershaw. Bregman followed suit, grinding out an epic 10-pitch plate appearance that won't soon be forgotten. It chased Kershaw from the game and set up the biggest swing of the Astros' season to that point.

The first man out of the Dodgers' bullpen was Kenta Maeda, who pitched 2 2/3 innings of scoreless ball in Friday's Game 3. He was tasked with facing Altuve, the toughest out in the Astros' lineup and one of the toughest in baseball. The AL MVP candidate worked the count full.

On the first full-count pitch he saw from Maeda, Altuve ripped a foul ball with home-run distance down the left-field line. On the next, he didn't miss. It traveled an estimated 415 feet out to center field and tied the game.

The emotional swing would be far from the game's last.

"Just when I thought I could describe Game 2 as my favorite game of all time," Hinch said, "I think Game 5 exceeded that and more." ∎

Game 6
October 31, 2017 • Los Angeles, California
Dodgers 3, Astros 1

L.A. TIE-UP

Astros Can't Get Their Traffic Home as Dodgers Beat Verlander, Force Game 7

By Jake Kaplan

After 179 games, the last 17 covering the three rounds of the postseason, the Astros' season will come down to one game.

The Astros lost to the Los Angeles Dodgers 3-1 on Tuesday night to set up a winner-take-all Game 7 of the World Series on Wednesday night at Dodger Stadium. Lance McCullers Jr. will start on regular four days' rest for the Astros opposite the Dodgers' Yu Darvish. But in reality, it will be all hands on deck for both teams.

This is the second consecutive season and the fourth time in seven years the World Series has required seven games to decide a winner. It will be the first Game 7 between 100-win teams since 1931, when the St. Louis Cardinals beat the Philadelphia Athletics. The 2017 season's final night will bookend what has been an all-time great Fall Classic.

"It's great baseball," Astros ace Justin Verlander said. "It's fun to be a part of. I wish we could've won (Tuesday night). But I've been a part of two of the best games I've ever played in, and they've both been in the World Series. That's pretty special. No matter what, this Series is going down in the history books as one of the best Series of all time.

"I think (Wednesday) is going to be nothing short of spectacular either way. I hope we blow them out. But just the way these things have been going, I don't see that being the case. It's going to be a battle. I think it's all hands on deck for both sides.

"When you have a great team with their back against the wall, and both of ours are, it's hard to beat them. And I think that's what makes Game 7 so special, especially in the World Series."

Although McCullers and Darvish will start, Wednesday night could see any pitcher on either staff pitch in relief, including the Dodgers' Clayton Kershaw

and the Astros' Dallas Keuchel. Maybe even Verlander, who threw 93 pitches in six innings Tuesday.

"We'll evaluate everything," Astros manager A.J. Hinch said when asked about Verlander's availability. "It would take a big effort, but you never know."

The Astros, who used only Joe Musgrove, Luke Gregerson and Francisco Liriano behind Verlander on Tuesday, will certainly have Charlie Morton and Brad Peacock as early options if McCullers falters early.

The Dodgers got through Tuesday without using Kershaw or Alex Wood. They extended closer Kenley Jansen into another two-inning outing but were fortunate in that he used only 19 pitches. They also again used relievers Brandon Morrow and Kenta Maeda, though.

"I don't ever think you practice as a kid for playing in three, four, five games in the World Series. It's always Game 7," Astros center fielder George Springer said. "And I know we lost (Game 6), but this is awesome to have a chance to come out here again. We'll see what happens."

To take down the Dodgers, the Astros will have to conjure the timely hits that eluded them in defeat Tuesday, when they were hitless in six at-bats with runners in scoring position against lefthander Rich Hill and four L.A. relievers.

"We knew going into this series it was going to be an absolute dogfight, a battle, and we're ready to meet them toe to toe again (Wednesday)," Astros third baseman Alex Bregman said.

Their Game 6 defeat marked the Astros' first in the 11 appearances (10 starts) Verlander has made for them since he was acquired in an Aug. 31 trade. Verlander was nearly unhittable for the first five innings but was undone by a hit by pitch and two timely Dodgers hits in the sixth.

Chris Taylor tied the score at 1 in the sixth with a

well-placed double off Verlander before Corey Seager put the Dodgers ahead with a sacrifice fly. Musgrove was first out of the beleaguered Astros bullpen. He allowed a Dodgers insurance run on a solo homer by Joc Pederson.

Jansen, the losing pitcher in the Astros' epic Game 5 walk off win Sunday night, shut them down in the eighth and ninth innings Tuesday.

Springer staked the Astros to a 1-0 lead when with two outs in the third inning he powered a Hill fastball the opposite way over the right-field fence. His fourth home run of the World Series matched a feat accomplished only 11 times previously, most recently by now-Dodger Chase Utley, who homered five times for the Phillies in 2009.

Since his 0-for-4, four-strikeout night in Game 1, Springer has homered in all but one game. All four have tied a game or put the Astros ahead. Since last season, Hinch has fielded questions as to why he leads off with probably his best power hitter. Springer's ability to spark a lineup like he did against the Dodgers is why.

The Dodgers' bullpen first stirred in the fifth inning. After Brian McCann led off with a single, Marwin Gonzalez moved him to third on a double down the left-field line. Hill struck out Josh Reddick and Verlander, at which point Dodgers manager Dave Roberts faced a difficult question: Should he let Hill face the top of the Astros' lineup a third time or turn to an overworked bullpen?

Roberts didn't deviate from the Dodgers' plan from Hill's previous postseason starts. After intentionally walking Springer to load the bases for Bregman, the Los Angeles manager walked to the mound to meet with Hill. When he took the ball from his starter, Roberts drew boos from the crowd. He called on Morrow to pitch for the sixth time in as many games.

Bregman had hit two balls hard off Hill, the first for a single. So when Morrow extracted from the Astros third baseman a weak ground ball to shortstop Seager, he bailed out Roberts from potentially endless criticism.

Hinch didn't need to worry much about third-time-through-the-order trends regarding his starter. Verlander overpowered the Dodgers with a fastball that averaged 96 mph. In the first five innings, he allowed only one runner on base, via a one-out single to center field by Yasiel Puig in the second.

But the third time through the order is the danger

zone for a reason, and upon their third look at Verlander, the Dodgers experienced much more success against the former MVP and Cy Young Award winner.

Austin Barnes led off the sixth inning with a single and became the Dodgers' first runner in scoring position when Verlander yanked a slider that bounced and hit Utley on the foot. Hinch walked briskly to the mound to meet with his pitcher, catcher and infielders before Dodgers leadoff man Taylor stepped into the batter's box for a third time.

Taylor swung and missed on a 1-and-1 slider from Verlander before smacking a 97 mph fastball. It found no man's land in shallow right field, allowing Barnes to score easily as the tying run and to leave Utley and Taylor in scoring position. Seager skied a sacrifice fly to the base of the wall in right field to give the Dodgers their first lead.

"I think when I sit down tonight and really reflect on this game, the one thing I'll be upset about was maybe falling behind Barnes (2-and-0), but he still didn't hit the ball very well, and that's baseball. He found a hole," Verlander said.

Verlander said he didn't want to get beat by Utley on what the pitcher described as "a mediocre slider." The slickness of the World Series baseballs, which pitchers have said affects their sliders, was in the back of his mind, he admitted.

"I'm not going to go home tonight and be like, 'Man, I pitched horribly,'" Verlander said. "I feel like I pitched pretty well, and I feel like a National League game dictated that I came out a little quicker than I probably would have."

Does that increase the low likelihood of Verlander's pitching in relief Wednesday? When asked about his potential availability, the 34-year-old righthander gave an answer that didn't suggest one possibility or the other.

"Right now I feel great, but I've got to sleep on it and see how I feel tomorrow," he said in the visitors' clubhouse after Tuesday's game.

If Verlander is available, it's unlikely anyone outside the Astros clubhouse will know until he begins to warm up in the bullpen. After the craziness of Game 2 and Game 5, perhaps a Verlander- or Keuchel-versus-Kershaw relief battle is the wrinkle in store for Game 7.

Said McCullers: "This series was destined to go seven pretty much the whole time." ■

Game 7
November 1, 2017 • Los Angeles, California
Astros 5, Dodgers 1

H-CROWN!

Astros Top Off Rebuild with First Championship in 56-Season History
By Jake Kaplan

Six years ago, on a Friday in November at the Astros' Union Station offices, Jeff Luhnow pitched new team owner Jim Crane his vision on how to fix the worst team in baseball.

It would be painful for a few years, and the Astros would have to remain patient and disciplined while enduring as drastic a teardown and rebuild as the sport has witnessed. But when the time was right, and enough elite prospects procured through the draft had matriculated from their farm system, they would compete for championships annually.

Through the years of losing, trading, selecting atop the draft and mining for hidden gems emerged the roster that delivered Houston its first World Series championship. At 8:58 p.m. Pacific time Wednesday night at Dodger Stadium, the Astros capped their franchise's 56th season with a 5-1 victory in Game 7 of the Fall Classic. The vision of Luhnow, their general manager, was realized.

"It made sense for us. Not every plan makes sense for every team. But where we started, with the worst team in baseball and one of the worst farm systems in baseball, we really had no choice," Luhnow said. "We had to focus on developing our own and, when the time was right, adding to it. That's what we did.

"We made some mistakes along the way. They're well-documented. But we had some hits along the way. Those are also well-documented. And here we are."

Luhnow spoke in a corner of the visitors' clubhouse at Dodger Stadium, home to the fourth and final champagne and beer celebration the 2017 Astros shared. The 51-year-old former St. Louis Cardinals executive, who came to baseball from the business world, wore black goggles atop his head and waded through the wreckage of the celebration with black Nike flip flops.

All across the room, players doused each other with beer and champagne. They smoked cigars. George Springer clutched the World Series trophy while a throng of reporters peppered him with questions.

Springer garnered World Series MVP honors after a historically great Fall Classic. The All-Star center fielder matched Reggie Jackson's and Chase Utley's record with five home runs in a World Series. He became the first player to homer in four consecutive games in the same World Series.

"It's unbelievable. It's indescribable," Springer said. "When you get to spring, you know who you have, you see what you have, and there's always that thought of, 'We could do it.' But the 162-plus games is a lot of games. And a lot of things have to go right in order to get here.

"And our team believed in each other all year. And through the good times and the bad times, through a rough stretch in August to getting down 3-2 against a very good New York (Yankees) team, there's a lot of things that happened. I'm so happy to be a part of it – to bring a championship back to a city that desperately needed one."

The Astros took Game 7 behind timely hits and a hodgepodge of pitchers, most notably Charlie Morton, their Game 4 starter who came out of the bullpen to pitch the final four innings.

Springer accounted for the first and last of the Astros' three hits against Dodgers starter Yu Darvish, who just as he did in Game 3 recorded only five outs before he was pulled. After his double down the left-field line to begin the game sparked a two-run first, Springer's 438-foot laser to left-center field punctuated a 5-0 lead for the Astros.

The young infield trio of (left to right) shortstop Carlos Correa, third baseman Alex Bregman and second baseman Jose Altuve were instrumental in delivering the first World Series championship in team history. (Brett Coomer/Houston Chronicle)

Nearly half of the Astros' dugout emptied onto the dirt track along the baseline when Springer's home run cleared the fence. Darvish had grooved a full-count, two-out fastball over the plate. His two terrible World Series starts sunk the Dodgers' chances.

For the first time in World Series history, neither starter completed three innings. A wild Lance McCullers Jr. was pulled after only 2 1/3 innings. But a mixture of McCullers, Brad Peacock, Francisco Liriano, Chris Devenski and Morton kept the Dodgers in check. Los Angeles was a woeful 1-for-13 with runners in scoring position.

The Astros have played 9,023 games since their franchise's inception in 1962. None featured higher stakes than Wednesday's.

The drama had only built over the first six games and 57 innings of an all-time-great Series.

"We're playing in one of the most epic World Series in history," manager A.J. Hinch said before Game 7, "and I think our players have appreciation for that."

Hinch didn't plan to address his team before Wednesday's game for that reason. After a 3-1 loss in Game 6, he was pleased with the vibe among his players, which he described as "the right amount of disappointment yet optimism toward Game 7."

By the time Darvish threw the game's first pitch, Hinch had ruminated for hours on the countless scenarios of how he could piece together 27 outs. He revealed little of his plans behind his starter but didn't rule out any of his 11 other pitchers appearing in the game.

In McCullers, the Astros had something of a wild card. A 24-year-old righthander whose fastball reaches the mid-to-upper 90s and whose curveball is among the best in the game, he has talent that is unquestioned. But in his Game 3 start, he had lost his command in a three-walk inning. It was uncertain which version would show up five days later.

The Astros got the erratic McCullers in Game 7, so much so that he set a record for any postseason game by hitting four batters. His shoddy fastball command prompted Hinch to pull the All-Star after only seven outs and 49 pitches.

Only because of his swing-and-miss curveball and mistakes by the Dodgers did McCullers not allow any runs. After stranding the bases loaded in a 25-pitch first, he survived the second because the Dodgers' Logan Forsythe strayed too far from second base on a Chris Taylor line out to Astros shortstop Carlos Correa, who easily turned two.

Peacock was first out of the Astros' bullpen. He finished the third, completed the fourth and recorded the first out of the fifth, an inning finished by Liriano and Devenski. Morton, in his first relief appearance since 2008, allowed the Dodgers' first run in the sixth on two singles and a walk. The Astros had nine outs to go.

Morton started the seventh and retired the Dodgers' No. 3, 4 and 5 hitters in order. He was perfect again in the eighth, so Hinch let him bat in the top of the ninth. The game – and the final out to clinch the Astros' first title – was Morton's.

Morton struck out Chase Utley on three pitches and induced a groundout to second baseman Jose Altuve from Taylor. On the first pitch he threw to Corey Seager, a 96 mph fastball, he got a groundout to the same spot. After receiving the throw from Altuve, Astros first baseman Yuli Gurriel threw his hands atop his head in disbelief.

"I just dropped down to my knees and realized a childhood dream came true," third baseman Alex Bregman said. "This team worked so hard for this. It's so special to be a part of this team. The coaching staff is unbelievable, ownership, our general manager, the city of Houston. We won this for them.

"I'll tell you this: We're very young, and we're going to be back next year looking to win another one."

In 2015, the Astros hired Hinch, who led them back to the playoffs ahead of schedule that October. The 43-year-old former major league catcher and front office executive is constantly lauded for his ability to connect with his players, who praise him at every turn.

"He pulled all the right strings. He really did," Luhnow said. "He's a great manager. He should be recognized as such, and hopefully, we'll be here next year doing the same thing."

Before Luhnow interviewed with Crane, who had then just recently purchased the team from Drayton McLane, he typed out a 22- to 23-page document of his plan for the Astros to achieve sustained success. A binder with those pages still sits in Crane's office. "I'm going to check it when I get back," Crane said Wednesday night.

At the end of his job interview, Luhnow asked Crane, "What are my constraints with this job?" Crane ripped off the top sheet of paper from a pad on his desk and tossed it to Luhnow, who expected a list.

The paper was blank.

"I can't ask for a better owner," Luhnow said Wednesday night, as a clubhouse full of World Series champions partied around him. ∎

After the final out of Game 7, Jose Altuve leaps into Carlos Correa's arms as George Springer races in from center field to join the celebration. (Michael Ciaglo/Houston Chronicle)

BY GEORGE!

Springer Hits Record-Tying Five Home Runs, Takes Series MVP Honor
By Jenny Dial Creech

When the grueling, thrilling, stress-filled seven games had ended, George Springer ran toward his teammates from right field. The Astros had just done it. They'd won the World Series.

As the leadoff hitter who was a constant force in the 2017 regular season, Springer put together a Fall Classic for the ages and celebrated the sweetness of victory after the Astros subdued a beast of a Dodgers team with Wednesday night's 5-1 victory in Game 7.

After the clincher was over, he stood on a podium in the middle of Dodger Stadium to collect the Willie Mays trophy, given to the Most Valuable Player of the Series.

"We did this for Houston," an emotional Springer said while holding the hardware and standing with his teammates, a World Series Champs hat sitting on his head. "We are coming home champions."

After the Series opener, some people were calling for Springer to be moved down in the lineup. He struck out four times in Game 1 against Clayton Kershaw and Kenley Jansen. Before that, he had hit .115 (3-for-26) against the Yankees in the American League Championship Series.

A.J. Hinch shrugged it off. The manager never worried about Springer, and neither did anyone else in an Astros uniform. They knew Springer would show up, that he would come through at the plate.

Springer didn't just prove naysayers wrong. He silenced them by becoming the best Astros player in the final six games of the season. On a team with so much talent, that is no small feat.

He hit five home runs – tying the record shared by Reggie Jackson and Chase Utley for a single World Series – including one in each of the last four games. He had extra-base hits in the final six games en route to 29 total bases – a record for any postseason series – and finished with a .379 batting average and 1.471 OPS in leading the charge past a 104-win Dodgers team.

Drafted in the first round in 2011, Springer was expected to play a key role for what was a rebuilding franchise. He made his Astros debut on April 16, 2014, going 1-for-5 with a walk against the Royals.

Before taking the field that night just hours after arriving in Houston – Springer went 3-for-4 with a grand slam and four runs the night before for Class AAA Oklahoma City – he told reporters he was trying to keep his cool in the biggest moment of his life.

"I wouldn't say that I'm (nervous)," Springer said. "Kind of the only way I can explain it: My coach at school would always say, 'You want to be like a duck. You want to be calm above the water, but underneath, his feet are just kicking and going and going and going and going.' So that's my plan: to be calm but just go out and play."

Since that day, Springer has certainly kept his cool, and he had huge moment after huge moment against the Dodgers.

His two-run, 11th-inning homer was the difference in the Astros' 7-6 victory in a classic Game 2 at Dodger Stadium. He tied their epic 13-12 triumph in Game 5 at Minute Maid Park with a homer that made it 8-8.

And after going deep for his team's only run in a disappointing 3-1 loss in Game 6, he started the Game 7 clincher with a double to ignite a two-run inning, then smashed a two-run homer in the second to put the Astros up 5-0.

George Springer hits a two-run home run off Los Angeles Dodgers starting pitcher Yu Darvish, his record-tying fifth homer of the World Series. The Astros tied the record for home runs in a postseason with 27 and set a World Series record with 15 homers. (Brett Coomer/Houston Chronicle)

Coming back to Dodger Stadium for a Game 7 with your back against the wall isn't easy. But Springer made it look that way out of the gate and set the tone for his team, which followed his lead.

When he missed 13 games with a quad injury in July and Carlos Correa missed 44 with a fractured thumb, Springer remained positive. When the Astros went through stretches where a number of their starting pitchers were injured, he didn't worry.

"A lot of things have to go right in 162 games," Springer said. "But we always believed. Through every stretch, through the tough times. And here we are. I always believed in this team."

Years before his name appeared in the World Series record book, the Astros saw something special in Springer.

Now the rest of the world has seen it, too. ■

Brett Coomer/Houston Chronicle

ROAD TO THE TITLE

SIMPLY A-MAY-ZING

Astros Match Best Month in Franchise History With 17-6 Romp Over Twins
By Jake Kaplan • June 1, 2017

Minnesota Twins reliever Ryan Pressly didn't even turn his head when George Springer connected with his elevated fastball. Left fielder Eddie Rosario hardly moved. The only uncertainty stemmed from whether the moonshot would reach Target Field's third deck or the upper reaches of its second.

According to MLB's Statcast, Springer's home run in the seventh inning of the Astros' 17-6 clobbering of the Minnesota Twins traveled an estimated 473 feet, the second-longest hit in the majors this season and barely shy of the third deck. The second of Springer's two homers on the afternoon, it kick-started a six-run frame that broke open the Astros' season-high seventh consecutive win.

In completing a three-game sweep of a series in which they scored a club-record 40 runs, the Astros capped their winningest month in 12 seasons. Their 22-7 record in May matched August 1998 and July 2005 as the best in club history. A third of the way through the regular season, the best team in baseball is on a 114-win pace.

"We've been doing it for two months. We need to do it for four more months," shortstop Carlos Correa said. "I think we're in a good position right now. But we're not going to get comfortable. We're going to strive for more."

Even playing a lineup minus three regulars in Josh Reddick, Carlos Beltran and Brian McCann, the Astros racked up a season-high 19 hits, including a season-high six home runs. Springer's blast was the farthest by an Astros player in the three seasons Statcast has tracked such data. It jumped off his bat at 112.6 mph.

Correa cemented his strong American League player of the month candidacy with his seventh home run of May, the most he's hit in any month of his three-year career. He also set career highs for a month in batting average (.386), on-base percentage (.457), slugging percentage (.673), total bases (68) and RBIs (26), three of which he collected on Wednesday.

Alex Bregman homered for the third consecutive game and for the fifth time in his last 10 games. Marwin Gonzalez hit his 12th home run of the season, Evan Gattis his fourth.

Springer, who batted from the designated hitter's spot for the first time this season, reached base in each of his six plate appearances and had a season-high four hits. The multi-homer performance was the fifth of his four-year career and second in 17 days. His first homer of the day, in the fifth inning off Twins starter Hector Santiago, traveled 381 feet to left field.

His second, to left-center field, trumped it by a long shot.

Ex-Astro Jason Castro had moments earlier narrowed the score to 6-5 with a two-run homer off Tony Sipp when Springer led off the seventh. Springer then took a strike and a ball before Pressly came at him with a 93 mph fastball up in the zone. The crack of the bat left no doubt.

"I was in shock," Correa said. "I've never seen a ball hit that hard before live in my life. It was not even really where it landed. It was just the way it sounded and the way it came off the bat. It skyrocketed off the bat. It was really impressive."

Only a 480-foot bomb by Jake Lamb of the Arizona Diamondbacks on April 29 at Chase Field outdistanced Springer's blast this season. Springer's previous longest this

Carlos Correa had a huge day at the plate, with three hits, three RBIs and a homer. The Astros routed the Twins, 17-6. (AP Images)

year was 454 feet on April 6 off the Seattle Mariners' Ariel Miranda at Minute Maid Park.

"That's all I've got," Springer said of Wednesday's blast. "That's about all I can hit it."

The next six batters after Springer in the seventh reached base as the Astros strung together five more runs. Gattis plated one on a ground-rule double. Yuli Gurriel scored two on a bases-loaded single.

After the Astros scored three more times in the eighth, the Twins had backup catcher Chris Gimenez pitch the ninth rather than waste another arm from their worn-out bullpen. Gonzalez took him deep for two runs, pushing the Astros past the season high of 16 they scored in Monday's series opener.

"This offense is a complete offense," Bregman said. "There's guys that can beat you in so many different ways. It's tough to navigate through an offense like this. It's pretty special to be a part of."

The Astros scored an ultra impressive 6.2 runs per game in May and have outscored opponents 62-28 during their winning streak. On Friday night against the Texas Rangers in Arlington, they will have a chance to improve to 23 games over .500 for the first time since the end of their 93-win campaign in 2001.

The season is just two months old.

"It's been special," Springer said. "The quality at-bat after quality at-bat in a row is something that I haven't seen before. So hopefully, we can keep this up." ■

CENTER FIELDER

GEORGE SPRINGER

Top-Notch Power

As Leadoff Slugger, Springer Flouts Baseball Convention
By Hunter Atkins • June 6, 2017

A lineup change on May 24, 2015, would prove later to be an innovation.

In the Sunday finale of a four-game Astros series at Detroit, George Springer, a second-year outfielder with sunken cheeks to complement a cleanshaven face, led off for the first time. He filled in for Jose Altuve, who usually batted first but had the day off following a 3-for-32 slump.

Anibal Sanchez began the game with a 91 mph fastball down the middle. Springer unleashed a swing so violent that he could have suffered whiplash. It was an emphatic whiff.

"I guess it would be safe to say," Alan Ashby said during the Root Sports broadcast, "George Springer is not your classic leadoff man."

He never would be.

In a game against the Rangers exactly one year later, Springer led off again, but he stayed put this time. He proceeded to bat first in 115 of the next 116 games.

Another year has passed, and the forgettable lineup change has developed into an unparalleled advantage for the Astros, who have the most wins and runs scored in baseball. No team has benefited more this season from a powerful first batter.

Springer, huskier and scruffier in his fourth season, had a stretch of seven homers in eight games preceding Monday's 7-3 win at Kansas City. One of those blasts soared 473 feet.

Springer catalyzed a sweep of the Rangers with his sixth leadoff home run of the season. He struck again in the fourth with his 16th homer overall and was named the American League's Player of the Week, having gone 15-for-30 with five homers, a double, 11 runs and nine RBIs.

"When he kick-starts us like that, there's an energy boost in our dugout," Astros manager A.J. Hinch said of Springer's penchant for leadoff homers.

Through Sunday, Springer ranked second in the AL in runs (43) and tied for eighth in RBIs (37). Those numbers rival Yankees right fielder Aaron Judge (44 runs and 41 RBIs). But Judge is a 6-7 cleanup monster - not a leadoff man.

"Stereotypes don't get very far with me," Hinch said.

The choice to begin the lineup with, effectively, a cleanup hitter became trendy last season. The World Series

George Springer flexed his huge power in 2017, crushing a career-high 34 homers. (Elizabeth Conley/Houston Chronicle)

featured the Cubs' Kyle Schwarber and Indians' Carlos Santana batting leadoff as designated hitters. The Orioles bumped up center fielder Adam Jones, and the Blue Jays tried slumping right fielder Jose Bautista at the top.

These men are built like nightclub bouncers, not base stealers. They get paid millions to cross home plate, not reach first base.

"Now the game is a lot different," said Altuve, whom Hinch installed in the No. 3 spot last year around the same time as Springer at leadoff. "It's about OPS."

OPS, the sum of on-base and slugging percentages, conveys the ability to get on base and hit for power. An OPS surpassing .800 is similarly admirable to batting above .300.

Springer's OPS was .895 entering Monday. Tampa Bay DH Corey Dickerson emerged this year as a new leadoff threat. His 76 hits led the AL and .979 OPS ranked fifth.

Springer has outperformed and outlasted his leadoff peers from 2016. After batting .190 when batting first this season, Schwarber was dropped to ninth. Santana hit .227 in 35 games leading off. Jones and Bautista no longer bat at the top.

When aligning hitters, Hinch imagines how they will perform in tandem.

"I do see some strengths in Springer when the lineup rolls around, which is not something you think of as a leadoff hitter," Hinch said.

It is easier to enjoy when Marwin Gonzalez bats seventh and posts a 1.034 OPS, eighth best in the AL through Sunday.

"The guys in the back of our lineup are the best in the entire league," shortstop Carlos Correa said.

Conventions that lasted a century reflected the scarcity of run-producing players. A first-inning run was treated as if it might be the last.

Not anymore. Leadoff hitters accounted for 10.3 percent of all home runs and drove in 9.6 percent of runs in 2016, both the highest such marks since 1920, according to Zack Kram of TheRinger.com.

"A 4-3 or a 5-4 game has replaced the 1-0 game," Springer said. "More teams are built to score every inning."

"I'm only going to bat first one time," he reasoned. "It's not necessarily a dying art, the art of the stolen base, but (opposing) teams would rather have you steal second than hit a three-run homer."

No need to ask the Rangers their preference. In Friday's 7-1 win for the Astros, Springer threw a tantrum after striking out in the sixth. He slammed his bat into the dirt and spiked his helmet. When bottom-of-the-order hitters Yuli Gurriel and Jake Marisnick got on base two innings later, Springer redeemed himself with a 444-foot home run to center.

The Astros' prolific run production has masked the rarity of multi-run homers for Springer: 11 of his 16 home runs have come without anyone on base.

The loss of potential run-scoring opportunities has not mattered for the best offense in the AL, but the theory that Springer would drive in more runs if he had more runners on base is closer to a guarantee. Altuve and Correa have batted with runners on base roughly 45 percent of the time, whereas Springer has done so 34 percent of the time and hit .333.

Springer had not led off regularly in youth ball, college or the minors. Now he is thriving as the first line of attack for the most potent arsenal of bats in the AL – even if he could be the biggest weapon behind hitters like Altuve and Correa.

His solo homers on Sunday did not move Hinch to consider moving Springer into the heart of the lineup.

"No," Hinch said. "No chance." ■

Springer watches his third-inning home run during Game 2 of the ALDS against the Red Sox.
(Karen Warren/Houston Chronicle)

CANADA HIGH

Astros Close First Half With Franchise-Record Rout, Pounding Blue Jays 19-1

By Hunter Atkins • July 10, 2017

It can happen quickly when playing against the Astros. A team looks comfortable. Its pitcher is in rhythm. It has two outs.

Then in a hurry, the Astros' lineup interrupts a sunny afternoon with heavy rainfall.

On Sunday, the Astros stormed the Blue Jays with a two-out, five-run blitz in the top of the second inning.

The Jays had, in theory, eight more chances to climb back. But the Astros surged for 14 more runs to overwhelm Toronto 19-1, putting an emphatic final stamp on a monumental first half of the season.

The Astros' 18-run margin of victory set a franchise record, surpassing the 17-run difference in an 18-1 win over the Cardinals on Sept. 20, 2007.

"That was incredible," manager A.J. Hinch said. "We never stopped."

The 18 runs were a season high for the majors' most potent offense, topping the 17 the Astros mounted against the Twins on May 30.

Amid a flood of 17 hits, Carlos Correa went 4-for-5 with two home runs and five RBIs. Jose Altuve, after a day off Saturday, had three hits for the fifth consecutive game, raising his major league-best batting average to .347. He scored three times and drove in three runs.

The Astros head into the All-Star break with 60 wins (against 29 losses), making them one of five teams to do so in the last 40 years (including this season's Dodgers, who are 61-29, and the 2003 Braves, 2001 Mariners and 1998 Yankees). Their run differential of 180 leads the American League by a whopping margin, with the Yankees second at 96.

The offensive outpouring could have compensated for poor pitching, but Brad Peacock (7-1) pushed through six innings as if he could have blown the lead on one bad offering. He struggled throwing low strikes on the outer edge and lost a feel for his curveball, but he undid his own jams in the fourth and sixth innings by inducing popups.

"Unreal," he said of his poor command. "I can't explain it. Sometimes it just happens. I lost it."

Despite giving up five walks and facing 27 batters, Peacock kept the Blue Jays off the board to underscore the lopsided game.

"This is a tough lineup, and he shut them down," Correa said. "He had a comfortable lead, and usually pitchers start getting sloppy and throwing pitches in the middle. He stayed composed."

The Astros have averaged 8.33 runs per game in Peacock's nine starts.

Yulieski Gurriel struck first in the second with his 11th home run. He lined the ball at such a low trajectory that he busted out of the box thinking it would not clear the wall.

The other blasts were not in question.

Jose Altuve watches the flight of his two-run home run off Blue Jays starting pitcher J.A. Happ during a dominant 19-1 win. (AP Images)

With two outs, Alex Bregman scored from second and George Springer reached first base on a smash that third baseman Josh Donaldson fielded well before overthrowing first base for a detrimental error.

Altuve followed with his 13th home run. He connected on a first-pitch changeup off J.A. Happ (3-6) and stepped out of the box slowly to admire the ball's flight to right field.

Correa put the Astros ahead 5-0 with his 19th home run. He adjusted to a low slider by bending his knee more than usual to square it up for a no-doubter. The ball catapulted off his bat at 107 mph and a 24-degree angle. Left fielder Steve Pearce did not take a step. He craned his neck to watch the ball hammer against the façade of the second deck.

"Nobody in the league is a better offensive team than we are," said Gurriel, who was used to being the best player on most of his past teams in Cuba. "To have three or four superstars, it takes a lot of pressure off me."

In the fourth, Correa drove in Bregman for a 6-0 lead, slashing a ground ball the other way. Second baseman Ryan Goins smothered it with a dive but did not have a shot to get a sprinting Correa at first.

Happ, who pitched four innings, was charged with only two earned runs because of Donaldson's error.

With the Rogers Centre roof peeled back, outfielders had to fight the sun in the third inning. By the sixth, an overcast sky darkened the field, and the Astros went ahead 9-0.

Springer and Altuve singled before Evan Gattis hit his eighth home run, besting Correa with his powerful rip. Not many home runs in the majors have cleared the wall in less than 4 seconds. Gattis turned on a high-and-inside fastball that went 403 feet in 3.9 seconds at 109 mph.

The Astros had lost on Thursday and Saturday. Hinch initially wanted to give Springer Sunday off, but the threat of the Astros losing their second road series of the year motivated the manager to start his best hitters the day before the All-Star break.

Hinch got to reprieve Springer when the Astros batted around in the seventh inning.

Jake Marisnick, Nori Aoki – substituted in for Springer – and Altuve drove in three runs on three hits to push the score to 12-0.

Correa, who hiked his batting average to .325, made it 15-0 with his 20th homer, a three-run shot that traveled 411 feet to center field.

It was the eighth time this season the Astros scored six runs in an inning. They hushed the crowd during their onslaught. Gattis inspired brief cheers when he grounded to short for the first out.

Marwin Gonzalez was left out of the action – until the ninth. After Gattis hit an RBI double, Gonzalez singled, and Correa scored on an errant throw from short. Gonzalez came around to score on a wild pitch for the Astros' final run.

For the second time in three days, Francis Martes came in to pitch the ninth inning and surrendered a home run.

The Blue Jays fans erupted with pent-up excitement when Ezequiel Carrera went deep. Their reaction was a touch exaggerated but appropriate given the absurd production they'd stuck around to watch. ∎

Carlos Correa celebrates hitting a three-run home run during the seventh inning of the Astros first-half finale. Correa launched 20 homers prior to the All-Star break. (AP Images)

CARLOS CORREA

He Stands Tall at Short

Correa Arrives at First All-Star Game as One of Baseball's Premier Players
By Jake Kaplan • July 11, 2017

On the bus ride from the players' downtown hotel to Marlins Park, Carlos Correa found himself surrounded by familiar company. George Springer sat to his side, Chris Devenski across the aisle. Jose Altuve, Dallas Keuchel and Lance McCullers Jr. were all nearby.

"I just felt like I was on the bus with the boys," Correa said. "I felt pretty comfortable."

Comfortable is also how the Astros star seemed when encircled by microphones and television cameras for roughly 45 minutes later in the afternoon. Although he's just 22 years old, the starting shortstop for the American League in the All-Star Game has been in the spotlight since the Astros drafted him first overall in 2012.

Long ago anointed as a potential perennial All-Star, Correa is making merely the first of what figure to be many appearances at the Midsummer Classic.

"It's something you want to do every year," Correa said. "You don't want to have a four-day vacation during the break. You want to be able to be part of this special team here. It takes a lot of hard work, and it takes a lot of

hits to be able to get here. Hopefully, I can keep doing it."

Correa, who will bat fifth for the AL, arrived at his first All-Star Game as one of the best players in baseball this season. While playing a premier defensive position, he ranks seventh in the majors in OPS (.979) and is tied for sixth in batting average (.325).

He closed the first half with four hits, two homers and a career-high five RBIs in the Astros' 19-1 rout of the Toronto Blue Jays. His 20 homers for the season give him six more than Francisco Lindor, the shortstop with the next most.

Correa, who already has matched his 2016 home run total, is one of only two shortstops in major league history to record three 20-homer seasons through his age-22 campaign. Alex Rodriguez is the other. His potential seems to have no limits. He's one of three MVP candidates representing the AL-leading Astros in Miami, along with fellow All-Star starters Altuve and Springer.

"It's honestly like he's matured 15 years in three years," Springer said of Correa's development as a player since the shortstop's June 2015 debut. "I don't really know how to

Carlos Correa cemented himself as a true star in 2017, making his first All-Star team, and batting .315 with 24 homers and 84 RBIs in only 109 games. (Karen Warren/Houston Chronicle)

describe it. He's an animal. He can hit for power. He can hit for average. He can hit the ball wherever he wants."

Correa and Altuve will become the first double-play partners to start for the AL since Robinson Cano and Derek Jeter in 2010, 2011 and 2012. It's not difficult to envision the Astros' up-the-middle duo repeating that feat for at least the next two seasons, the last two of Altuve's current contract.

"It's really special to share the field again with Altuve, a guy I've learned so much from and a guy that makes me better every single day just by playing next to him and watching the way he works," Correa said. "It's going to be really special to share the field in the All-Star Game with him."

McCullers has been a teammate of Correa for all but a matter of days since the Astros made the two of them their top two picks in general manager Jeff Luhnow's first draft rebuilding the team. They advanced through the minor leagues together and debuted in the majors within a month of one another in 2015.

"Every year that I've played with Carlos, from 2012, I've been able to see him not only take steps (but) like leaps and bounds to become that player that everyone thinks he can become and will become," McCullers said. "He is that player right now."

As a kid in Puerto Rico, Correa watched the All-Star Game every summer and dreamed of eventually playing in it. He said he also dreamed of attending a Home Run Derby, which he did Monday night. He watched alongside Lindor from the area in front of the first-base dugout with the rest of the AL All-Stars.

"It's surreal," he had said earlier of his first All-Star experience. "It's something that will be with me for the rest of my life, to be able to be here in my first All-Star Game, start at shortstop for the American League, and be able to share this special moment with my family." ∎

Correa slides safely home off of a hit by Yuli Gurriel during Game 1 of the ALCS, a 2-1 Astros win. (Elizabeth Conley/ Houston Chronicle)

HOUSTON STRONG

Astros Put City, Victims Front and Center in Sweeping Mets
By David Barron • September 3, 2017

The 1969 Astros were jesting as they sang pitcher Larry Dierker's ditty about their slapdash squad, "It Makes a Fellow Proud to Be an Astro." Against the Mets at Minute Maid Park, the day's emotions were expressed by a uniform patch with the team logo, an outline of Texas and the word "Strong."

It's a public expression of the genuine pride the 2017 Astros have this season and beyond for their wounded city.

In their post-Hurricane Harvey return to downtown Houston, Josh Reddick and Marwin Gonzalez had RBI singles and scored during a four-run sixth inning, lifting the Astros to a 4-1 win over the Mets in the nightcap of the first Houston doubleheader since 1999 at the Astrodome.

In the opener, the Astros pounded out 17 hits in a 12-8 win before a crowd that included evacuees, volunteer relief workers and first responders.

Reminders of Hurricane Harvey's toll were everywhere to be seen. Players wore the new uniform patch, and pitcher Joe Musgrove threw 2 1/3 innings of two-hit relief work in the nightcap wearing shoes autographed by young evacuees he met at the George R. Brown Convention Center.

The Astros wore their emotions on their sleeves, too. Manager A.J. Hinch told the crowd, "Stay strong, be strong, go 'Stros," and outfielder George Springer pointed to the "Strong" logo on his chest after hitting a two-run home run in the opener.

"There are thousands of people who don't have homes, don't have belongings, and they are rallying around us," Springer said. "And it's our job as the sports team to do anything we can ... to provide anybody with some sense of relief, some sense of break."

The Astros chipped away in the nightcap, trailing 1-0 through five against Mets starter Seth Lugo (5-4) before tying it on base hits by Alex Bregman and Reddick, sandwiching a walk to Jose Altuve, and taking the lead when Altuve beat the throw home on Gonzalez's single to right.

Reddick scored on a groudout by Brian McCann, and Gonzalez went from first to third on the play and scored on J.D. Davis' sacrifice fly.

Musgrove and closer Ken Giles shut down the Mets the rest of the way, and Musgrove said he drew strength from footwear and fans.

"We felt like we were carrying everybody in our hearts," Musgrove said. "Having the shoes on my feet is a constant reminder of what some people are going through and how fortunate we are.

"It was a special day for everybody, and we were glad to pull out both wins for the fans."

In the opener, the Astros exploded off Mets starter Matt Harvey for seven runs in two innings and got an effective starting job from Charlie Morton (11-6), who allowed six hits and struck out nine in five innings.

It was an emotional weekend of baseball back at Minute Maid Park as the recovery from Hurricane Harvey was just beginning. (Karen Warren/Houston Chronicle)

"You want the game to lift people up. You want to do right for the city," said Morton, one of 16 players who visited evacuees Friday.

"I'm really proud to be an Astro. I'm really proud to be a small part of this city and this community."

Springer had two hits with a home run, two RBIs and two runs scored in the opener. Altuve had three hits with three runs scored and an RBI and Gonzalez and Reddick each drove in two runs.

Harvey (4-4), just off the disabled list with a stress injury to his right shoulder, had the shortest start of his career, allowing seven earned runs on eight hits in two innings.

"Playing the game, that is what we do," Hinch said. "We were ready to play. We can separate everything leading up to today after the first pitch. Seven runs in the first two innings, a manager will never complain about that."

Houston sent eight to the plate in the first inning, highlighted by Gonzalez's two run double. Springer's two-run homer came in the second, and Reddick had a two-run base hit in the fourth, followed by Davis' solo home run.

Morton was touched up only for a two-run homer by the Mets' Dominic Smith in the fourth. The bullpen struggled once more, capped by a five-run seventh inning that included a grand slam by Wilmer Flores, but the Astros added two in the seventh, including a RBI single by Tony Kemp.

The Astros will depart after the series finale for a road trip that will include the debut of Justin Verlander, who arrived in Houston during the first game, threw a bullpen session between games and received one of the day's biggest ovations when the El Grande video screen briefly showed him in the Astros dugout.

Verlander joins a team that has struggled of late but still has the best record in the American League, clinched their third consecutive winning season with the sweep of the Mets and now has a new source of inspiration.

"I want so badly to do well for these people, and I want our team to do well for our people," Springer said.

Springer was asked at what point when he was rounding the bases after his homer he started thinking about Hurricane Harvey's flood victims.

"I haven't stopped," he replied. ■

Houston mayor Sylvester Turner shakes hands with first responders before throwing out the first pitch prior to the start of the Astros' game against the Mets. It was the first professional sporting event in the city since Hurricane Harvey. (Karen Warren/Houston Chronicle)

STARTING PITCHER

JUSTIN VERLANDER

Trade Secrets

Inside the Final Hours that Brought Justin Verlander to the Astros
By Jake Kaplan • September 17, 2017

On the morning of Aug. 31, the day he would make the hardest decision of his baseball life, Justin Verlander woke up not expecting anything to happen.

The face of the Detroit Tigers for more than a decade, Verlander figured he would finish his 13th major league season with the only team for which he'd ever pitched. Before the July 31 non-waiver trade deadline, the Tigers had dealt outfielder J.D. Martinez, catcher Alex Avila and relief pitcher Justin Wilson. It seemed like any other significant moves would wait until winter.

Aug. 31 represented the final day teams could acquire players and have them eligible for inclusion on their postseason rosters. If Verlander wasn't traded before 11 p.m. Central, he would simply finish out his season with Detroit. The rumor mill would calm until November.

Little did Verlander know that he would be pacing around his living room with less than 45 minutes to decide where he would pitch the remainder of this season and the next two. The 34-year-old righthander says he doesn't like to make any decision rashly. This situation would render it nearly impossible not to.

"(Tigers general manager Al Avila) had talked to me a lot throughout the process, and I knew that the Astros had contacted and were probably the most serious threat," Verlander would say a week later when recounting the frenzy of that night. "But still, it was never presented to me in a way that made me think that something was actually going to happen.

"So I just never really thought about it. That was my only way to continue to go about my job in Detroit. If I'm going to heavily think about (trade possibilities), then I'm not going to be doing my job on the mound. It was just kind of background noise until all of a sudden."

All of a sudden, a potential Hall of Fame pitcher was tasked with a career-altering decision, one that signaled the official end of an era for the team with which he will always be synonymous and injected him into a pennant race for another, one that had the former MVP and Cy Young Award winner donning a new uniform just two days later.

Seventeen days later, Verlander will make his first home start for the Astros. Sunday afternoon's series finale against the Seattle Mariners will be the Minute Maid

Justin Verlander was one of the best pitchers in baseball during his tenure with the Tigers, earning a Cy Young Award, MVP, Rookie of the Year Award and six All-Star selections. (Karen Warren/Houston Chronicle)

Park faithful's first opportunity to watch the man whose addition not only improved the Astros' odds to win in the postseason but helped lift a city recovering from the devastation of Hurricane Harvey.

All because of a late-night Aug. 31 blockbuster that came down to the final seconds.

Verlander was home that day at his apartment in the Detroit suburb of Birmingham. It was a Thursday, and the Tigers were off. He had pitched the day before, throwing six innings of one-run ball at Colorado's Coors Field, the latest outing in a resurgent second half. It would come to signify the last of his 380 regular-season starts sporting the old English D.

In the afternoon, word of a move that would set in motion the events of the evening popped on Verlander's radar via social media. Seemingly out of nowhere, the Tigers had traded All-Star outfielder Justin Upton to the Los Angeles Angels. Verlander sent a text message to Avila, the Tigers' GM, to gauge where things stood for him.

Talks were ongoing, he was told, but no deal was probable. So Verlander continued to go about his off day.

On the other side of the country, Astros general manager Jeff Luhnow went through countless waves of increasing optimism and growing pessimism.

By Aug. 31, he had been in the Los Angeles area for a week, unable to fly back to Houston after a series the Astros played in Anaheim the same weekend Harvey made landfall. Luhnow's wife's parents live in L.A., so on that Thursday morning he set up shop at the dining room table of his in-laws' Brentwood home.

Luhnow and Avila had ongoing negotiations preceding the July 31 non-waiver trade deadline, a day after which Luhnow was widely criticized for his failure to execute a significant deal. At one point on Aug. 30, Luhnow felt pretty confident a deal for Verlander would get done. By day's end, he considered the probability pretty low.

On the morning of the 31st, Luhnow had another deadline to tend to first. The claim the Astros had won two days earlier on Los Angeles Angels outfielder Cameron Maybin was set to expire late in the morning Pacific time, and the teams had yet to work out a deal.

With minutes remaining before the claim expired, the Angels agreed to send Maybin to the Astros as long as they took on the roughly $1.5 million left on his $9 million salary for this year.

Luhnow didn't know at the time the Angels agreed to part with Maybin because they had acquired Upton from the Tigers, a deal that would in turn help facilitate the Verlander trade. At the time of the Astros' Maybin acquisition, Luhnow said, he didn't think they would land Verlander.

Luhnow's wife, Gina, had made a dinner reservation for that evening at 8:15. With 45 minutes until the deadline, Luhnow figured, the Astros would have either made a trade or know negotiations were dead.

"I woke up probably pretty pessimistic that anything would happen," Luhnow said. "At one point early in the morning California time, I became much more optimistic. Then it waned again, and I became pessimistic. That cycle continued about every couple of hours, and sometimes there were just minutes between cycles. It was pretty intense.

"Knowing that the clock was ticking all along and recognizing that we had a lot of pieces to put in place even if there was agreement, it started to get pretty stressful I'd say around 6 p.m. Pacific time."

At 6 p.m. Pacific, Luhnow oddly enough found himself at the "Bad News Bears Field" in West L.A., where he had promised his 11-year-old nephew he would watch his Little League practice. His nephew's coach asked Luhnow to speak to the team. All the while, the GM was in the middle of negotiations for one of the biggest trades in Astros history.

"The whole thing was a little surreal," Luhnow said. "I'm at a Little League practice with 11-year-olds, giving

Having spent his entire career with the Tigers, Verlander was reluctant to leave Detroit, but it turned out to be a championship-caliber decision for him and the Astros. (Karen Warren/Houston Chronicle)

them a talk about how to practice. Meanwhile, this deal's going on in the background."

Negotiations between the Astros and Tigers had intensified in August, a month in which Verlander reeled off strong start after strong start and the first-place Astros struggled. The Detroit ace cleared trade waivers early in the month, an expected formality given the $56 million in guaranteed money he's owed over the 2018 and 2019 seasons.

Through July, Verlander had a 4.29 ERA in 22 starts. By August's end, he had improved it to 3.82. He had also dominated the major league-leading Los Angeles Dodgers for eight innings of one-run, two-hit ball on Aug. 20. The Astros, meanwhile, played their worst in August, an 11-17 slog on the heels of their relative inactivity – they did acquire lefthander Francisco Liriano from the Toronto Blue Jays – at the July 31 trade deadline.

In addition to the Astros and Tigers needing to find common ground on a prospect package, they had to agree on how to divvy the rest of Verlander's contract. According to people familiar with the negotiations but not authorized to speak publicly, the Astros earlier in August offered to pay $18 million annually of the $28 million Verlander will make in 2018 and 2019. That was $2 million below Detroit's asking price.

The Astros later conceded to paying $19 million per year. When on Aug. 31 Luhnow and Avila agreed to the prospect package the Astros would send the Tigers – highly touted 19-year-old righthander Franklin Perez, outfielder Daz Cameron and catcher Jake Rogers – Astros owner Jim Crane gave the go-ahead for the final $1 million needed to meet the Tigers' ask.

Luhnow was back at his in-laws' house getting ready for dinner when he and Avila agreed the deal was done. But then came the uncertainty over whether Verlander, who has full no-trade rights, would say yes. Luhnow asked his wife to push their dinner reservation to 9:00 or 9:15 p.m. Pacific.

Back in Michigan, Verlander and fiancée Kate Upton had gone for a late dinner at about 9:30 p.m. Eastern, still not expecting a trade. But as they made the roughly five-minute walk home from The Bird & The Bread restaurant at about 11:20, Verlander's phone rang. It was Avila.

"And then I had to make the hardest decision I've ever had to make in baseball," Verlander said.

Verlander's conversation with Avila was brief. The gist: There was a deal in place, and the pitcher had to decide if he would accept. Once back at his apartment, Verlander began making calls, many of them back and forth with his agent, Mark Pieper.

"Given that period of time, I just wanted to get as much information as I could, whatever it was," Verlander recounted in an interview with the Houston Chronicle. "'What are we talking about in two years? What are we talking about right now? What's the locker room like? What are these guys like? What's the town like? … There was just a hurricane there. Obviously, they're in bad shape as a city. What's that like? Can I live somewhere?' Stuff I hadn't even thought of. I was just trying to weigh all of that."

Within this short window of time, Verlander received a call from Astros ace Dallas Keuchel, who had heard the trade rumblings while back at his apartment in Houston. The Astros had landed in Houston earlier that evening after playing the last of their three "home" games against the Texas Rangers in St. Petersburg, Fla. It was their first night home since Harvey hit.

"'Hey, I'm not trying to take too much of your time up. You won't regret your decision to come here,'" Keuchel recalled this week of his message to Verlander. "'Obviously, your window for winning in Detroit is damn near closed, and ours is wide open.'

"I figured the only thing left in his legacy is to win a World Series, because he's pretty much done everything else. I was hoping that would resonate in his mind rather quickly, and I think it did."

Verlander was spectacular in his five regular-season starts with the Astros, winning all five games and striking out 43 in 34 innings, with a 1.06 ERA. (Karen Warren/Houston Chronicle)

Ultimately, Verlander has said, his decision came down to the opportunity to win. The Tigers' trade of Upton earlier in the day signaled a full rebuild in Detroit. If that move doesn't happen, the Verlander trade probably doesn't, either.

"You're looking at our team (in Detroit) thinking, 'We still have a decent core of guys here. It's not a full rebuild. Who knows what can happen with the right pieces in place?'" Verlander said of his mindset at the time. "And I made these comments: I said, 'As long as I'm wearing a Tigers jersey, I plan on winning with the Tigers.'

"I was still looking at it from a very optimistic point of view of 'We've got guys that if the right pieces fall into place, we can still win.' And then when (Upton) goes, then it's kind of like, 'I don't think that's possible anymore.' That definitely was one of the things on my mind in the decision-making."

Verlander doesn't remember the exact time he made the decision to accept the trade. It couldn't have been much earlier than 11:50 p.m. Eastern, 10 minutes until the deadline, he said.

"I knew in my brain that I had all of the information. I had everything that I was going to have," he said. "I'm not exactly sure what time it was, but it was late, and in the middle of one of my paces I look at Kate and go, 'Screw it. We're going to Houston.' And she goes, 'OK!' and got excited. It was a pretty cool moment, really."

Avila, who according to a Tigers spokesman wasn't available to comment for this story, had planned ahead and sent baseball operations officials to Verlander's apartment with the necessary paperwork for the pitcher to sign.

As part of accepting the deal, Verlander retained his full no-trade rights and also asked the Astros to void the $22 million option for 2020 that would have vested if he finished among the top five in AL Cy Young Award voting in 2019. Verlander, who continues to defy the aging curve, viewed it as essentially a club option. If he places in the top five, he will be worth much more than $22 million on the open market in the 2019-20 offseason.

Once that was hashed out, Verlander signed, and a photo of the document was emailed to the MLB commissioner's office for approval.

"I don't know how this would've worked before cellphones," Verlander said.

The trade required MLB approval because of the money changing hands between the teams. When midnight Eastern time hit, Luhnow was in the dark as to whether the deal had actually gone through in time. It was out of his hands at that point. There was nothing more he could do.

On his and his wife's 10-minute drive to dinner, Luhnow sat in the passenger's seat in the hopes he would receive a franchise-altering phone call from MLB. At about 9:15 p.m. Pacific, 15 minutes after the deadline, it came. The deal was done.

After he hung up with the commissioner's office, Luhnow sent word to Crane and then to Astros manager A.J. Hinch, who was on the back patio of his home in The Woodlands catching up with his wife, Erin, after a hectic week. Hinch texted his coaches. Already asleep by then, Astros pitching coach Brent Strom awoke to the news in the middle of the night.

At last, Luhnow sat down at The Brentwood Restaurant & Lounge feeling like he "just went through a traumatic experience." He ordered a cocktail – Tito's and soda with a lime – to unwind and celebrate.

"It tasted great," he said. ∎

It was all smiles at Justin Verlander's press conference following the trade to the Astros. He turned out to be the missing piece in the team's quest for a World Series title. (Karen Warren/Houston Chronicle)

THE WEST IS WON

Astros Clinch First Division Title Since 2001

By Jake Kaplan • September 18, 2017

At about a quarter after 5 p.m., after the final champagne-soaked player had left the field and headed back into the clubhouse, the last of the couple hundred Astros fans who stayed behind trickled up the stairs toward the Minute Maid Park exits.

They had remained in the sections directly behind the Astros' dugout for more than an hour after shortstop Carlos Correa caught the final out of Sunday afternoon's 7-1 victory. On the day their team clinched its first division title in 16 years, they stayed to witness the celebration.

For some, it was their first. Before these Astros clinched the American League West in their 149th game of the season, 16 years had elapsed since the franchise had last won a division title. Sunday's win sealed the team's second postseason appearance in three seasons and to the organization served as validation for long, hard years of rebuilding.

"We wanted to do it in front of our home fans," lefthander Dallas Keuchel said. "I had been joking before that the clubhouse (attendants) wanted us to do it on the road because they didn't want us to trash the clubhouse.

"But to clinch in front of our home fans, who have supported us the last couple years as we've gotten better and better, it just means the world. We're hoping to lock up some home-field advantage as well so we can get some more home crowds behind us."

By number of games, this year's team was the fastest of the Astros' seven division-winning teams to clinch. At 91-58, they are 15 games better than the AL West's second best, the Los Angeles Angels. Since even May, the celebration that took place Sunday seemed only a matter of when, not if.

"One of the messages I gave our team is, 'You never know if you'll be on a better team ever,'" Astros manager A.J. Hinch said. "'You've got to enjoy this because it's hard to do.' We won the division this year. The Astros haven't won the division since 2001. That shows how hard it is to win in this league.

"There are teams around the league that have expectations and don't live up to it. There are teams that surprise. We went wire to wire with expectations, and it feels pretty good to finish the job that we started."

Appropriately, the Astros closed out the division with Justin Verlander on the mound. In his first home start for his new team, the newly acquired ace righthander struck out 10 in seven innings of one-run baseball. Hinch called on Chris Devenski and Ken Giles to close out the win despite the lopsided score.

After Giles allowed three consecutive singles, he induced a game-ending popup that Correa tracked into his glove at 4:01 p.m. The All-Star shortstop, one of four Astros to homer in the game, clapped his right hand

George Springer hugs Jake Marisnick, with a cast on his hand, as they celebrate on the field after clinching the American League West crown by beating the Seattle Mariners 7-1. (Karen Warren/Houston Chronicle)

against his mitt three times. The players, those already on the field and those who were in the dugout, mobbed each other behind the pitcher's mound.

Blue T-shirts and hats commemorating the division title were handed out on the field to players and coaches. Players and coaches hugged. Minutes later, the players ran down the first-base line to high-five fans. They crossed the field and did the same down the third-base line before retreating to the clubhouse.

Once in the clubhouse, they doused each other with bottles of Korbel and Budweiser. The furniture had been cleared out, the lockers covered by plastic sheets. Outfielder Josh Reddick hugged Astros general manager Jeff Luhnow while wearing an American flag speedo. The relievers wrapped bullpen catcher Carlos Munoz in duct tape.

"There's no need to hold back," Reddick said.

Players and coaches lit cigars. Some Facetimed on their iPhones with family members. Outfielder Jake Marisnick walked around with saran wrap covering his right arm. He was only two days removed from surgery to repair a fractured right thumb.

It was a scene of pure jubilation.

"The stage of my career that I'm at right now, I came here for this reason. I came here to win a world championship," catcher Brian McCann said. "This is step one.

"The type of players we have on this team, we love to show up to the ballpark. We love each other. We play for each other. We have a group of older guys. We've got a group of younger guys. We've got some guys who are in the middle, and everybody produces. It's just a great dynamic."

By about 4:50 p.m., the players were back on the field with their families as the fans who remained in attendance cheered. When Jose Altuve sauntered back toward the dugout, fans chanted, "MVP. MVP. MVP." Keuchel and Verlander were two of the last to head back inside for more celebrating.

"For us, this is just the beginning of it," Correa said. "We've still got bigger goals." ▪

Justin Verlander waves to fans after the team clinched the AL West. Verlander was the winning pitcher in his home-field debut. (Elizabeth Conley/Houston Chronicle)

22
RIGHT FIELDER

JOSH REDDICK

Spidey, Speedo and Splendid Production

Reddick is Big on Fun, but Seriously, He Can Play
By Brian T. Smith • September 22, 2017

He is the 912 area code (Savannah, Ga.) thickly tattooed in black on his left arm.

He's the Spider-Man logo on his T-shirt and webbed superhero costumes proudly hanging inside the locker of a 30-year-old man.

He's the king of the woos, who celebrates hard by wearing only an American flag Speedo, then puts on an American eagle shirt when the cameras zoom in.

He also crashes into walls, runs out grounders, guns out would-be advancers, and entered Thursday evening at Minute Maid Park tied for the team lead in RBIs.

There really is no way to fully capture Josh Reddick in a few paragraphs.

But one quote from manager A.J. Hinch says everything about just how essential No. 22 has become for the 2017 Astros.

"The most underrated player on our team, to be honest," Hinch said before his club went for a three-game sweep of the White Sox. "He's not getting near enough love for what he brings to the ballpark every day."

There are perfect fits. Then there is Reddick.

He hits behind leadoff man George Springer and ahead of should-be MVP Jose Altuve, blending precision and line-drive power at the plate. He plays with the passion, electricity and fun that defined the young 2015 Astros but has nine years of MLB experience and 64 postseason at-bats, which will soon be critical for the '17 team. He can teach the younger Astros and regularly messes with Springer, another Hinch favorite. But Reddick's also still young enough to look left in the clubhouse and realize the importance of sitting next to 40-year-old Carlos Beltran.

"He's crazy," said Hinch, using that word as a compliment. "He blends in perfectly. On a team of really big, fun personalities, he might be the biggest, and he might be the most fun. And it comes out every now and then, especially during celebrations."

"Speedo," Reddick said. "It's not a bikini. It's a Speedo."

When the Astros signed the Savannah native to a four-year, $52 million free-agent deal last November, the move was applauded but not universally praised.

Josh Reddick celebrates in his signature American flag Speedo after the Astros 4-0 win over the Yankees in Game 7 of the ALCS. (Karen Warren/Houston Chronicle)

Reddick hit 32 home runs for Oakland in 2012 and batted .364 with the Dodgers during a National League Championship Series defeat to the eventual World Series champion Cubs in 2016.

But he was also limited to 115 games or fewer in three of his previous four seasons, and he spent his initial three pro years trying to prove himself in Boston.

In 132 games with the Astros, Reddick has gone from initially proving himself against lefthanders to a locked-in outfielder and one of Hinch's most trusted weapons. His .316 batting average is a career high and ranks second on the team behind the MLB-leading Altuve. Reddick's .851 OPS is also a career high, and he's fourth on the club in runs (77) and games and fifth in on-base percentage (.365).

"The comfort level since getting here has been fantastic, and I knew I was coming to an already good team," Reddick said. "My goal was just to come here and try not to screw things up."

Becoming a critical part of the second-best team in the American League has allowed Reddick to be himself even more.

During those three seasons with the Red Sox, Reddick played an average of 47 games and was surrounded by big-name proven veterans: David Ortiz, Jason Varitek, Kevin Youkilis, Josh Beckett, Dustin Pedroia.

"In Boston, I kept my mouth shut. … I was the only young guy," Reddick said.

He came of age in Oakland, winning a Gold Glove and finishing 16th in AL MVP voting during his first season with the Athletics in 2012 – and growing a mountain man-like beard that makes Dallas Keuchel's look like a trimmed mustache.

Reddick injured his wrist early during the next season by crashing into a Minute Maid wall and never regained his full '12 form.

"I should have shut it down right away," he said. "It was hurting so bad, and I just kept trying to play through it."

Reddick credited former A's teammate Coco Crisp for teaching him when to speak up and when to "keep my mouth shut."

As his first season in Houston has unfolded, the man who was showered with "woos" during his first-inning at-bat Thursday – Reddick's walk-up music is simply the trademark expression of former wrestler Ric Flair – has felt more and more at home at Minute Maid.

"That's me," Reddick said. "What you see is out there. What you saw in the (AL West title) celebration. What you see now is what you're going to get. This is a childhood dream still for a lot of us, and I'm going to enjoy it."

As for the famous swirling sound that will only grow louder in October?

"Going back to that first homestand, it's just crazy that fans would even start doing that randomly," Reddick said. "I turned around, and I was like, 'That's kind of weird.' Because I know Texas is a big wrestling state. … But I didn't expect it to be a WWE field event, where people are just wooing around.

"I went home and talked to my buddy. I said, 'Man, if they're out there like that, imagine if I walked up to it the next day.' Sure enough, here we are months later, dealing with it. But it's been great, because it shows you how much they want to get into it."

Springer and Reddick constantly get into it – for fun.

"I love it. He's been awesome here," Springer said. "He's always on my case. He's always on everybody's case. It's funny."

Hinch and Reddick text almost nightly after games, with the Astros' right fielder still going over the previous game.

"I'm proud he's on our team," Hinch said. "He signed here for this reason – to be on a playoff team – and he's contributed much more than people talk about."

Three hours before Keuchel threw the first pitch Thursday, Reddick was already into it. The man with the 912 tattoo, Spider-Man costumes and American flag Speedo was hunched in front of a computer, breaking down old at-bats in a makeshift tunnel space between the Astros' clubhouse and dugout.

It was another part of Reddick, just as real as all the rest. ■

Reddick was a force in the lineup in his first year with Houston, hitting .314, with 13 homers and 82 RBIs. (Karen Warren/Houston Chronicle)

27

SECOND BASEMAN

JOSE ALTUVE

The Crown Fits Him

Altuve Wraps Up Third Batting Title in Four Years
By Jake Kaplan • October 2, 2017

Jose Altuve's winning the American League batting title has become so much the norm that there was little attention or fanfare surrounding the latest accomplishment of the Astros' star second baseman. The fact it has become basically expected is perhaps the best indicator of Altuve's greatness.

"Going into any year, I would say most experts would expect him to win the batting title," Astros manager A.J. Hinch said before the AL West champions finished their 101-win regular season with a 4-3 victory over the Red Sox. "Which is insane to think about, given how many good hitters there are in the league."

Altuve wrapped up batting championship No. 3 and his third in four seasons with a major-league best .346 average in 590 at-bats. The clip set a career high and was the best by an Astro since Moises Alou hit .355 in 2000. Altuve batted .341 when he won his 2014 batting title and .338 last year.

The Astros plan to toast their AL MVP candidate in the clubhouse after the pre-American League Division Series workout at Minute Maid Park.

"This one is a little bit more special. This is the first time I win a batting title and the team is going to go to the playoffs," said the 27-year-old Altuve, who joined Miguel Cabrera (four) and Joe Mauer (three) as recent AL players to win at least three career batting titles. "I'm just trying to do everything I can to help this team."

Altuve is the first major leaguer to win back-to-back batting titles since Cabrera won three straight from 2011-13. Between the two of them, a Venezuelan has won the AL batting title in seven consecutive seasons. A Venezuelan has won in either league for eight straight years, as Colorado's Carlos Gonzalez was the 2010 NL batting champion. Altuve takes pride in that.

"I feel happy to be part of that small group," Altuve said.

White Sox right fielder Avisail Garcia, also from Venezuela and a friend of Altuve, finished second in AL batting at .330. Charlie Blackmon of the Rockies won the NL batting title with a .331 clip. Blackmon led the majors in hits with 213.

"Starting from tomorrow, everybody's going to go from zero," said Altuve, who after batting leadoff Sunday

Jose Altuve had another incredible season for the Astros, hitting a major-league best .346, while slugging 24 homers, driving in 81 runs and stealing 32 bases. (Karen Warren/Houston Chronicle)

will move back to the third spot in the Astros' lineup for the postseason. "Zero wins. Zero losses. Your average is zero. So I've got to try to do the same thing to help my team to win."

Altuve's .346 average is the third best in a single season for an Astros player who had enough plate appearances to qualify for the batting title. Hall of Famer Jeff Bagwell batted .368 in his 1994 NL MVP season, which was strike-shortened. He finished second in the NL in average that season to Tony Gwynn (.394). Alou's .355 in 2000 also placed him second, behind Todd Helton (.372).

Altuve, who went 0-for-2 with two groundouts to third base Sunday, finished a double shy of 40 for the season. His 204 hits were 12 more than the AL player with the next most, Kansas City's Eric Hosmer.

The consistency with which Altuve accomplished his cumulative average is incredible. He batted .347 before the All-Star break and .344 after it. He hit .345 against righthanders and .353 against lefties.

The biggest discrepancy is his home and road splits. Altuve batted .311 at home and .381 on the road. No regular player has recorded that high of a road batting average since Ichiro Suzuki's .405 in 2004.

Altuve also became the first player in major league history to lead his league outright in hits four consecutive seasons. Suzuki led the AL in hits for five consecutive seasons from 2006 to 2010 but tied with Dustin Pedroia in 2008.

"It's crazy to think of how routine he's making 200 hits a year. We just sort of expect that, and it's not easy," said Hinch, who refers to Altuve as "the heart and soul of what we're about."

"It's not easy to be as consistent as he's been." ∎

Altuve's consistent excellence early in his career has him on a similar Hall of Fame path as Astros legend and fellow second baseman Craig Biggio. (Karen Warren/ Houston Chronicle)

FIRST BASEMAN

YULI GURRIEL

Great Import

Accustomed to the International Stage as a Cuban Star, Yuli Gurriel is Thriving
By Jenny Dial Creech • October 13, 2017

It's not rare to look around Minute Maid park during Astros games and see the wigs.

Sprouts of light brown hair sticking straight up.

The wigs are great, but nothing compares to the real thing.

Yuli Gurriel's signature hairdo makes its appearance from time to time after he delivers a big hit and takes off his batting helmet.

The grin a few inches below has become as beloved as the pineapple-shaped hair.

Since joining the Astros late last season, Gurriel has become an instant hit among fans. And teammates. And the rest of the American League.

Gurriel might still be relatively new to the majors, but the 33-year old is not new to baseball.

He has played on big stages internationally for years, so it's no surprise he is excelling in the playoffs now.

Heading into the American League Championship Series opener against the Yankees, Gurriel, who retained his rookie status this year has been one of this postseason's best performers. He has nine hits in 17 at-bats (.529) over four games and has struck out just once. (Or 15 times fewer than New York rookie sensation Aaron Judge in six games.)

When Gurriel signed with the Astros last July, it was a big moment for a team that for years had been building toward winning big. Committing $47.5 million over five years to the Cuban star showed just how serious the Astros, a franchise on the rise, were about pursuing a championship.

Expectations were high for Gurriel, but his progress and gradual adaptation to the majors has been impressive.

After slashing .262/.292/.385 in 130 major league at-bats a year ago, Gurriel upped those figures to .299/.332/.486 in 2017 and increased his home run total from three to 18. His 43 doubles led the Astros and tied for seventh in the majors.

A.J. Hinch would like to say he knew what all he was getting with Gurriel, but the Astros manager laughs when he thinks about how much better Gurriel has been than he could have imagined.

"I didn't know he was going to get multiple hits in every game in the postseason," Hinch said. "But I think his ability to handle the stress and anxiety that comes with the situations is not surprising. He's been on the international stage. He's been the central sports figure of a country

From his memorable hair to his lively personality, Yuli Gurriel has been a hit on and off the field for the Astros. (Karen Warren/Houston Chronicle)

where baseball is beloved, so I think his personality that has come out this year, his exuberance, his overall consistent play has been something we've expected. It's nice to see it play out."

In addition to what he's done offensively, Gurriel has been impressive at first base. He switched to the position from third and hasn't skipped a beat.

"I think his adjustment at first base is sort of glossed over," Hinch said. "His work around the bag – he's turned into one of the best scoopers at first base on balls in the dirt. His range is really good. We could move him to the other side, but we don't have to. But that's not easy to take an international star and put him at first base – a position he has rarely played – and end up rather good at it."

Gurriel said he has found a level of comfort with the Astros. He has enjoyed getting to know his teammates, has a great relationship with them and, in the midst of that, is having a blast playing the game.

Through a translator, Gurriel said he's not surprised how he has adjusted to playing in the United States and that he is happy with the transition.

The more comfortable he gets, he said, the better his play gets.

What might be the most impressive part of what Gurriel has done so far is the fact he has yet to bend under any pressure. In Game 3 of the ALDS, he became the first Cuban-born player to collect four hits in a postseason game. In the Game 4 clincher at Boston, he tripled, doubled and singled.

He never seems fazed. And when things start going well – the way they have in his postseason at bats – he gets rolling.

Gurriel said his confidence picks up when he gets a hit, and he feels even better when he goes back to the plate. He also feeds off his teammates, and lately, he said, everyone has been playing really well.

Gurriel has found a home with the Astros, and they couldn't be happier about it. He's comfortable in his own skin and on their roster.

And in wearing that unmistakable hairdo. ∎

The 33-year old rookie's defense at first base has been better than expected and his power has carried over from his days in Cuba, hitting 18 homers during the 2017 season. (Brett Coomer/Houston Chronicle)

PLAYOFFS

Game 1
October 5, 2017 • Houston, Texas
Astros 8, Red Sox 2

BOOM! BOOM! BOOM!

Altuve's 3 Homers Highlight Win Over Sale in Opener

By Jake Kaplan

Each of the four times he stepped into the batter's box, Jose Altuve was serenaded with chants of "MVP" from the Minute Maid Park crowd of 43,000-plus.

The Astros' superstar second baseman used three of those at-bats to author the signature performance of his career.

Altuve's legend grew in Game 1 of the American League Division Series between the Astros and Boston Red Sox. In his team's 8-2 win, the five-time All-Star and 2017 AL MVP candidate became the ninth player in major league history to hit three home runs in a postseason game.

All three were solo blasts, each more unbelievable than the last. The first two came off Boston lefthander Chris Sale, one of the best pitchers in baseball. His third prompted a curtain call. Forget the postseason. No Astros player had homered three times in a regular-season game in a decade.

"That was amazing to watch," said shortstop Carlos Correa, who bats behind Altuve in the relentless Astros' lineup. "He made me feel like a leadoff hitter today."

Altuve became the first player to homer three times in a postseason game since Pablo Sandoval, his fellow Venezuelan, did it in Game 1 of the 2012 World Series for the San Francisco Giants against the Detroit Tigers. Others to accomplish the feat include Albert Pujols, Adrian Beltre, George Brett, Reggie Jackson and none other than Babe Ruth, who did it twice.

Altuve's heroics highlighted a 12-hit day for the Astros, who will send Dallas Keuchel to the mound for Game 2 of the best-of-five series. Their Game 1 pitcher, Justin Verlander, had ample run support in his 17th career postseason start. Sale, the Red Sox ace, was charged with seven runs in his first exposure to October ball.

"I think we can officially call him a 'run producer,'" Astros manager A.J. Hinch said of Altuve. "I think in a lot of ways he gets so many hits that I think some of his run production gets cast aside a little bit.

"But he's the best hitter in the league, and that's in a league of really, really good hitters. And to watch him have a day like today, it's a great reward for the work that's put in to not only be a good hitter who gets hits but be a good hitter who produces runs, and that's not easy to do at this level."

Altuve, who's listed at 5-foot-6, 165 pounds but will refer to himself as 5-foot-5, 160, said he had never before in his life had a three-homer game. He homered 24 times in each of the last two regular seasons. In this latest one, the best of his seven, he posted a .957 OPS. But in typical Altuve fashion, he used his postgame press conference to deflect attention to his teammates.

"What happened today is new for me," he said, "and I'm really happy that it happened in a playoff game."

Baseball's best offense broke out early behind its raucous orange-clad audience. Alex Bregman and Altuve went deep back-to-back off Sale in the first. Marwin Gonzalez cracked a two-run double in the fourth. Between

Jose Altuve and Carlos Correa celebrate Altuve's fifth-inning home run. The Astros' second baseman hit three solo homers in his team's 8-2 win over the Red Sox. (Brett Coomer/Houston Chronicle)

Altuve's two other home runs in the fifth and seventh, Brian McCann plated two runs on a single in the sixth.

Against Sale, Altuve launched fastballs registering 97 mph and 95 mph, both left over the plate, out to almost the exact same spot in left-center field. On his third homer, this one to left, Altuve capitalized on an 83 mph changeup Red Sox rookie righthander Austin Maddox threw to the middle of the strike zone.

After each of his homers, Altuve was met in the dugout by the outstretched arms of teammate George Springer. After the third, Springer jokingly grabbed at Altuve's right biceps.

"He's a joke," Springer said. "He said he's never hit three homers in a game in his life. That's a great day to hit three. The dude's a 'create a player.' He's the MVP of the league. I don't see who else could be. He's unbelievable."

Sale, a six-time All-Star and an AL Cy Young Award candidate, recorded only 15 outs. He gave up nine hits, three of which left the park. The Astros ran his pitch count to 75 through four innings. He exited after yielding the second of two Evan Gattis doubles and a Josh Reddick walk to begin the bottom of the sixth.

Verlander wasn't his best but was more than good enough in six innings of two-run ball. The 34-year-old righthander struck out only three and walked two. Fifth and sixth innings of eight and 12 pitches, respectively, helped him overcome a pitch count of 79 through four innings.

For Altuve, his three long balls matched his hit total from his disappointing 2015 ALDS against the Kansas City Royals. He joined former Anaheim Angel Adam Kennedy as the only second basemen in history with a three-homer game in the playoffs.

The last three-homer game by an Astro in the regular season came courtesy of Carlos Lee on April 13, 2007, against Philadelphia. Carlos Beltran in Game 5 of the 2004 NLDS and Correa in Game 4 of the 2015 ALDS were responsible for the only previous two-homer postseason performances in Astros history.

"I told him the last time I've seen three home runs in a game was Pablo Sandoval, and I gave up two of them, so I'm glad there's somebody new that's done it," Verlander quipped. "But the guy, Jose, he's an incredible baseball player." ■

Justin Verlander put up six solid innings for the Astros, starting opposite Chris Sale in Game 1. (Karen Warren/ Houston Chronicle)

Game 2
October 6, 2017 • Houston, Texas
Astros 8, Red Sox 2

ACCORDING TO PLAN

Correa Picks Up Where Altuve Left Off, Backs Solid Start by Keuchel

By Jake Kaplan

A.J. Hinch hasn't had to tax his bullpen, make a tough substitution or really render any difficult in-game decisions 18 innings into this American League Division Series. Through the first two games, it's been all Astros.

A second consecutive 8-2 victory in Game 2 leaves the Astros needing to win only one of three games against the Boston Red Sox to advance to the ALCS. Their first chance to clinch their first postseason series since the 2005 NLCS will come in Sunday afternoon's Game 3, when Brad Peacock will start opposite ex-Astro Doug Fister at Fenway Park.

Charlie Morton would start for the Astros in Game 4 if one is necessary. If Game 3 follows a script anything close to that of Game 1 and Game 2, it won't be.

"We won't take anything for granted," said Hinch, the third-year Astros manager, whose team flew to Boston on Friday night and will work out there Saturday afternoon. "This is a team that's very, very laser focused on winning the series. You don't win the series with two wins; you win it with three."

The same offense that led the majors in slugging percentage while being the hardest to strike out has been on display in full force in the first two games. In addition to outscoring the Red Sox 16-4, the Astros have out-

homered them 6-0. They are batting a collective .343 and slugging .686.

"It shows the depth of our team," said outfielder George Springer, who led off the bottom of Game 2's third inning with a home run. "It's not the same guy every day. Except it's always (Jose) Altuve day."

Altuve, the AL's three-time batting champ and potentially its 2017 MVP, had two more hits in Game 2, only this time both were singles. The first, with two outs in the first inning, set the table for a two-run blast over the Crawford Boxes by Carlos Correa. The second, in the third inning, drove in Alex Bregman and put the Astros up 4-1.

The Red Sox chose not to pitch to Altuve in his third and fourth plate appearances, intentionally walking the second baseman each time to instead face Correa. Altuve has reached base safely in seven of his nine plate appearances in the series, which he kick-started with his epic three-homer performance in Game 1.

"To be honest with you, I came to the ballpark mentally prepared for that situation," Correa said of Boston's intentionally walking Altuve. "He hit three homers (in Game 1). He's the best hitter in the game right now, so I was expecting when the first base was open, there were guys on base and in an important situation, he was going to get walked."

Shortstop Carlos Correa launches a home run off Boston's Drew Pomeranz in the first inning of Game 2 at Minute Maid Park. (Michael Ciaglo/Houston Chronicle)

Fittingly, Correa delivered the biggest swings of the afternoon for the Astros in Game 2. On top of his first-inning homer off Drew Pomeranz, he broke open the game with a two-run double off Addison Reed in the sixth. It was the 23-year-old shortstop's second career four-RBI postseason game after Game 4 of the 2015 ALDS.

"I think it all starts with the starting rotation. When you have two Cy Young winners in the front of your rotation, it gives you a lot of confidence, and we in the lineup know that a couple runs will be enough," Correa said. "So it's good to start with an early lead, and then (Justin) Verlander and (Dallas) Keuchel are going to do the rest.

"We know that if we can go out there and score early, we're giving them a good chance to feel comfortable out there on the mound."

In a postseason of short outings, the Astros have had each of their top two starters pitch into the sixth. A day after Verlander tossed six innings of two-run ball, Keuchel completed 5 2/3 and allowed only one run.

Keuchel recovered from a rocky start to retire 13 consecutive batters between the second and sixth innings before a walk of Hanley Ramirez spelled the end of his day. The former Cy Young Award winner surrendered only three hits.

"They had a good game plan early on, and that was to look over the plate and raise their eye sights, and I wasn't able to pull up the two-seam," Keuchel said.

"So I just went to plan B, and that was go extreme – extreme in with the cutter and slider – and was able to get some early strikes, get ahead in the count, attack them and kind of put them back on their heels and was fortunate enough to make an adjustment early enough before it was too late."

The Astros knocked out Pomeranz in the third inning. Their performance marked the first time in Astros history they've scored eight runs or more in consecutive postseason games. No team had scored eight runs or more in multiple games in the same Division Series since the 2012 St. Louis Cardinals did it three times in five games against the Washington Nationals.

"We couldn't really script it any better," Keuchel said. ■

George Springer (4) and Jose Altuve (27) celebrate at home plate following a two-run double by Carlos Correa. (Karen Warren/Houston Chronicle)

Game 3
October 8, 2017 • Boston, Massachusetts
Red Sox 10, Astros 3

FLIES IN THE OINTMENT

Reddick Has Homer Taken Away, but Devers Crushes One Off Liriano

By Jake Kaplan

Rafael Devers, the 20-year-old lefthanded-hitting third baseman for the Boston Red Sox, accumulated 240 plate appearances in his rookie season. Only 57 came against lefthanders. But in those 57, Devers mashed.

So when Astros manager A.J. Hinch pulled righthanded starter Brad Peacock in favor of inconsistent lefthander Francisco Liriano in the third inning Sunday, it qualified as a questionable move. When Liriano hung an 0-and-1 slider over the plate and Devers clubbed it 430 feet to right-center field, the decision became the misstep that loomed largest in a 10-3 Astros loss in Game 3 of their American League Division Series with Boston.

Devers' swing put the Red Sox ahead 4-3, a score that represented their first lead of a to-that-point one-sided ALDS. It was a lead the Red Sox wouldn't relinquish, extending the best-of-five series to a fourth game. The Astros will start righthander Charlie Morton in their second attempt to clinch. The Red Sox will counter with righthander Rick Porcello.

On Sunday at Fenway Park, the Red Sox broke open a tight game with a six-run seventh inning. David Price emerged as their hero on the mound, pitching four scoreless innings of relief. A vaunted Astros lineup that romped for eight runs in each of the team's Game 1 and Game 2 victories was silenced for the final eight innings of Game 3.

"Price was really good today," Astros shortstop Carlos Correa said. "You've got to give credit to the guy when he pitches the way he pitched today. His cutter was very sharp, and he was working off of that. He did his part. You've got to tip the hat."

While Price dominated for the Red Sox, Lance McCullers Jr. matched him for three of those four innings in his first career relief appearance. In the seventh inning that doomed the Astros' chances at a comeback, McCullers allowed the first two runners to reach base before an uncharacteristic meltdown by Chris Devenski.

Devenski allowed two singles and a double, the latter of which came off the bat of Hanley Ramirez and plated two runs. Ramirez, whom the Red Sox benched in Game 1 in favor of Eduardo Nunez, went 4-for-4 with three RBIs in the game.

Devers also drove in three runs and had two hits, none bigger than his home run off Liriano.

In his 57 regular-season plate appearances against lefthanders, Devers batted .400 with a 1.074 OPS. Liriano held lefthanders to a .247 average and .655 OPS in 100 regular-season plate appearances. If Hinch was set on pulling Peacock, Devenski and his .111 average and .414 OPS against in 157 plate appearances versus lefthanded hitters seemed the best option at the time.

When he got his chance later, though, Devenski didn't even record an out. Hinch summoned Joe Musgrove to try to clean up the mess. Musgrove allowed a three-run homer to nine-hole hitter Jackie Bradley Jr., who got an assist off the outstretched glove of right fielder Josh Reddick.

Josh Reddick narrowly misses a chance to rob Jackie Bradley Jr. of a three-run home run. After dominant showings in Games 1 and 2, Reddick's Astros found themselves at the wrong end of a 10-3 score line at Fenway Park. (Karen Warren/Houston Chronicle)

"The ball kept curling over. I had enough time to get over, I thought, and timed the jump pretty well. Just in and out," said Reddick, who was robbed of a three-run homer in the second inning by Red Sox right fielder Mookie Betts.

"It's just one of those things where it doesn't go your way, and it is very unfortunate for myself and the team. But nothing you can do. You get one taken away from you, and you give one right back. It's just one of those things where it doesn't go your way."

In all, the Astros' bullpen was charged with seven of Boston's runs. Three were charged to Devenski, two to McCullers, and one apiece to Liriano and Musgrove. Peacock was charged with the other three. He completed only 2 2⁄3 innings.

Hinch pulled Peacock after a two-out double by Mitch Moreland and a run-scoring single by Ramirez on which the Boston designated hitter took second on an error by left fielder Marwin Gonzalez. Hinch called on Liriano, who had a 4.40 ERA in 14 1⁄3 innings of relief for the Astros in the regular season despite September improvements.

The Astros liked the matchup of Liriano's power fastball and slider against the bottom of the Red Sox order: Devers, the switch-hitting Sandy Leon, and the lefthanded-hitting Bradley. But after spotting a 94 mph two-seamer down and in for strike one, Liriano left an 87 mph slider over the plate.

"That pocket down there at the bottom, we felt pretty good about Liriano, the way his power should work against the bottom of the order," Hinch said. "He hung a slider, which didn't work."

Devers, who turns 21 on Oct. 24, became the youngest player in Red Sox history to hit a postseason home run and joined Mickey Mantle, Andruw Jones, Miguel Cabrera, Manny Machado and Bryce Harper as the only players to homer in the playoffs before their 21st birthday.

Said Liriano: "I didn't execute the pitch, and it stayed right down the middle. He put a good swing on it."

Through a half-inning, it appeared the Astros would trounce the Red Sox as they had in the first two games of the series.

Two batters and two minutes into the game, they led 1-0 on singles by George Springer and Reddick, with a Doug Fister wild pitch mixed in. Correa, the fourth batter of the game, made it 3-0 with a blast to dead center field on a full-count curveball Fister left up in the zone.

The homer signified Correa's second of the series and already the 23-year-old's fourth in his postseason career. Only Carlos Beltran (eight), Lance Berkman (six) and Mike Lamb (five) have accounted for more postseason home runs in Astros history.

Red Sox manager John Farrell afforded Fister only the first time through the Astros' order before he replaced him with Joe Kelly, who recorded the next five outs, one on the deep fly ball off the bat of Reddick that would have cleared the three-foot right-field wall had Betts not snagged it.

Then came time for Price, the $217-million man and former Cy Young Award winner who has yet to surrender a run in 15 1/3 innings during his temporary tenure as a reliever.

"I don't think there are a ton of secrets," Hinch said. "I don't think there's a ton of strategy change other than I like the way we jumped out ahead. Obviously, we could have jumped out even further ahead if we had two more feet on Reddick's ball or if he hits the ball in the corner a little bit more.

"But our attack plan's going to be the same. We're going to be fine. We'll bounce back out of this and come back and play hard. But this is playoff baseball. If anybody thought the Red Sox were going to lay down, probably rethink it." ◼

Hanley Ramirez celebrates a two-run double off Astros reliever Chris Devenski during the seventh inning. The Astros bullpen allowed seven runs in what was a do-or-die game for the Red Sox. (Karen Warren/Houston Chronicle)

Game 4
October 9, 2017 • Boston, Massachusetts
Astros 5, Red Sox 4

BOSTON GLEE PARTY

Bregman, Reddick Help Clinch Series With Big Hits in 8th-Inning Rally
By Jake Kaplan

In the smallest visitors' clubhouse in the major leagues, it seemed not a soul who entered between 5 and 6 p.m. local time exited unscathed. Upon almost every sighting of dry clothes, a player or coach corrected the issue with a dousing of beer and champagne.

For some, celebrating the Astros' first postseason series win since 2005 came with a feeling of redemption. For others, it was validation. For all, it meant the preservation of one of the best seasons in franchise history.

The Astros advanced to the American League Championship Series by virtue of a wild 5-4 victory over the Boston Red Sox in Game 4 of the American League Division Series on Monday afternoon at Fenway Park.

The appearance in the LCS will be the Astros' first as members of the American League and their first in either league since 2005, the year they made their lone World Series appearance after winning the National League pennant.

"We envisioned ourselves being here since the beginning of the year, and nothing really changes on our end," Astros third baseman Alex Bregman said. "We're going to keep showing up to the yard every day, having fun, competing, playing the game the right way, playing it hard, and playing for each other."

Monday's clincher had a little of everything, including light rain throughout. Both teams' aces, Justin Verlander for the Astros and Chris Sale for the Red Sox, made surprise multi-inning relief appearances. Carlos Beltran,

the oldest player on the field, was responsible for what became the decisive swing. Bregman, among the youngest on the field, tied the score with a homer.

Four hours and seven minutes had elapsed when Astros first baseman Yuli Gurriel secured in his mitt the throw from second baseman Jose Altuve for the final out. After celebrating in the clubhouse for close to an hour, the Astros retook the field in front of an empty stadium to snap a team photo. They flew back to Houston later in the evening.

"This is such a hard place to play," Astros manager A.J. Hinch said of Fenway Park. "I don't think it gets the credit of being a really, really tough (place to play). These fans know baseball, they know their moments, they know how to have the home-field advantage.

"So when we get to this park, we didn't assume anything. We didn't think we were just going to come in easily and win a game. We know how tough it is to play here."

After winning Games 1 and 2 by identical 8-2 scores, the Astros lost Game 3 10-3. When Andrew Benintendi cracked a two-run homer off Verlander in the fifth inning of Game 4, it felt like the momentum in the series had shifted. Benintendi's big swing put the Red Sox up 3-2 in the game.

By the time the eighth inning rolled around, Sale had dominated for four consecutive frames. The AL Cy Young Award candidate had allowed only two hits and struck

Third baseman Alex Bregman rounds the bases in the eighth inning after taking Boston's Chris Sale deep. Houston's late rally was key in securing a trip to the American League Championship Series. (Karen Warren/Houston Chronicle)

out six without walking a batter. He complemented his usual wipeout slider with a fastball he ran up to 99 mph. His stuff was filthy.

But to lead off his fifth inning of work in the eighth, he attacked Bregman with changeups. Bregman was ready for them, and when Sale left one over the plate, the 23-year-old delivered the biggest hit of his young major league career with a game-tying solo blast over the Green Monster in left field.

"I had all the confidence in the world that we were going to find a way to scratch and claw like we have done all year and get the lead back," said Bregman, who hit a first-inning homer off Sale in the series opener. "I was in the dugout, and (bench coach) Alex Cora came up to me and said, 'Hey, one at-bat. That's all that matters.'

"I was 0-10 going into that (over) my last 10 at-bats. And he said, 'One at-bat. That's it. Have some fun. Play the game how you did the beginning of the series, just having fun.' I was fortunate enough to get a good pitch to hit and put a good swing on it."

Evan Gattis then kick-started the go-ahead scoring opportunity when he smacked a one-out single down the left-field line. Cameron Maybin came in to run for him. With two outs and George Springer coming to the plate, Boston replaced Sale with arguably the best closer in the league, Craig Kimbrel. Springer drew a two-out walk.

Then came the most impressive at-bat of the day. Tasked with hitting a 99 mph fastball or a 90 mph curveball, Josh Reddick fouled off four pitches before getting a 99 mph heater he smacked the other way into left field. Maybin, who was running on the full-count pitch, scored what was then the go-ahead run.

As Reddick rounded first base, Fenway Park fell silent. Later, the veteran outfielder celebrated as he did when the Astros clinched their division – wearing only an American Flag speedo.

"If we keep doing this," he said, "I may ride the parade in this thing."

Ken Giles, called upon for a six-out save, shut down the Red Sox in the eighth to set the stage for the Astros' offense to tack on in the ninth. With two outs and runners on first and second, Hinch pinch-hit Beltran for Maybin against Kimbrel. Like Reddick the inning before, Beltran saw eight pitches. The last of them was an 87 mph curveball Beltran clanked off the Green Monster for a run-scoring double.

Ken Giles gets doused in beer and champagne by teammates after recording the save in the Astros' ALDS-clinching win in Boston. (Karen Warren/Houston Chronicle)

That insurance run loomed large when Rafael Devers led off the ninth with an inside-the-park home run on a fly ball that caromed off the Green Monster into center field. Giles recovered to retire the final three batters, finishing off the game by inducing a groundout to Altuve from Dustin Pedroia.

Beltran's double represented the 40-year-old's 200th career postseason at-bat. He improved his impressive playoff average to .325.

"He's Mr. Clutch," Astros shortstop Carlos Correa said. "There's nobody better in the postseason who's active right now than him. So we expected something good to happen there."

The Astros batted .333 (49-for-147) with a .402 on-base percentage in the ALDS, each a franchise best for a postseason series. Their pitchers had a 4.63 ERA, but Boston's had a 6.35. The Astros' Championship Series appearance will be just the fifth in the franchise's 56-season history.

"It's a little bit like a redemption feeling," righthander Lance McCullers Jr. said. "We were six outs away in '15, man. We were six outs away from the ALCS. The team that beat us (the Kansas City Royals) ended up winning the World Series. It was tough for everyone. It's still been tough for everybody. So just to be able to close it out and to go in the ALCS and give the fans this time to enjoy, it's pretty cool." ∎

Opposite: Alex Bregman watches his game-tying homer clear the fences. Above: Astros bullpen coach Craig Bjornson wasn't spared the champagne shower treatment in Fenway Park's visitors' clubhouse. (Karen Warren/Houston Chronicle)

Game 1
October 13, 2017 • Houston, Texas
Astros 2, Yankees 1

SPECIAL K

Keuchel Fans 10, Extends Mastery Over Bronx Bombers
By Jake Kaplan

It doesn't seem to matter which players Joe Girardi writes into the New York Yankees' lineup. Whether the last generation of Bronx Bombers or this new one, Dallas Keuchel has proved to be their kryptonite.

Keuchel reprised his role as a Yankee killer on his biggest stage yet Friday night: Game 1 of the Astros' first League Championship Series in 12 years. In the first of four wins his team requires to advance to the World Series, this one by a 2-1 margin, the bearded lefthander delivered perhaps his best start of the season.

"I think that's the most locked in I've seen him maybe all year," Astros third baseman Alex Bregman said. "Maybe even better than a few of the starts that he had early in the year."

Not only did Keuchel pitch seven scoreless innings, he did it against a Yankees lineup that produced the second-most runs in the majors during the regular season. Not since his Cy Young Award-winning campaign in 2015 had he struck out 10 batters like he did in Game 1 of this ALCS. He had the best version of his sinker and his swing-and-miss slider.

Keuchel's strikeout total was the highest by an Astros pitcher in a postseason game since Hall of Famer Nolan Ryan struck out 12 in Game 5 of the 1986 NLCS against the Mets. Keuchel is just the second pitcher in history after Hall of Famer Bob Gibson to record seven strikeouts or more in his first four career postseason starts.

In front of a raucous, orange-towel-waving crowd of 43,116, Keuchel rose to the occasion.

"When the sinker is moving and the gun is hitting 90," Astros shortstop Carlos Correa said, "I know he's going to be lights-out."

Keuchel's latest gem improved his career numbers against the Yankees to a 1.09 ERA in eight starts, including two in the playoffs. In 57 2/3 innings against baseball's most storied franchise, he has not allowed a home run.

In Friday's Game 1, he didn't allow even a double. The Yankees managed only six baserunners in his seven innings, four on singles, one on a walk and the other on a bobbled grounder by Jose Altuve. Keuchel threw 109 pitches, his most since April, before he walked off the mound at 9:35 p.m. and was met on the dugout steps by the right hand of Astros manager A.J. Hinch.

"There's really no hard explanation for it," Keuchel said of his success against the Yankees. "I think it's just pitch execution, and it's just been there more times than it hasn't against the Yankees.

"But the Yankees are so storied. It's just a storied franchise, and they have so much rich history that you almost don't even have to get up for the game. You're already up for it."

To complement his 10 strikeouts, Keuchel induced eight outs on the ground. His trademark sinker featured the late life it does when he's at his best. He supplemented it with cutters, which he has used increasingly since late in the regular season. His slider was as effective as it's been

Jose Altuve connects for a sixth-inning single in what was a slim 2-1 victory over the New York Yankees. (Karen Warren/Houston Chronicle)

since he returned in late July from the neck issue that cost him eight weeks of the season.

"Sinker, cutter, slider. He didn't even use a changeup today. He's got so many plans out there, and when plan A is working, he sticks with it, and when plan A doesn't work, he goes to plan B," Correa said. "That's what makes him so special."

Said catcher Brian McCann, "He pitched an incredible baseball game."

The legs of Altuve, the bats of Correa and Yuli Gurriel, and the arm of Marwin Gonzalez did the rest.

Altuve, serenaded by the crowd at his every move by "MVP" chants, had three more hits and manufactured the game's first run in the fourth with his legs. After reaching on an infield single up the middle to second baseman Starlin Castro's back hand, he stole second base. On the next pitch from Masahiro Tanaka, Correa lined a single to left field to score his double-play partner.

Correa advanced to second on a groundout by Gonzalez and scored on a single by Gurriel. The Astros' three singles in the inning accounted for all but one of the hits they mustered off Tanaka, who completed six innings as the other half of a pitchers' duel. Tanaka surprised the Astros by throwing only 16 splitters among his 89 pitches, an abnormally low total for him.

In a low-scoring game, it was appropriate that a defensive play changed the complexion of the evening. Gonzalez, an infielder playing left field, saved a run for Keuchel in the fifth. After a leadoff single by Greg Bird and the error by Altuve, Keuchel got Todd Frazier to fly out and struck out Brett Gardner to put himself on the verge of escaping the jam.

But with two outs, Aaron Judge lined a single to left field. Yankees third-base coach Joe Espada sent Bird, and Gonzalez threw a strike home just in time to get him.

Later, it loomed large.

"You can't really say enough about the play of Marwin the whole season," Keuchel said. "He's literally the most undervalued player in the big leagues. And now that we got national attention, we're seeing everybody's worth." ■

Dallas Keuchel's masterful seven-inning performance was essential in the Astros' Game 1 ALCS victory. (Karen Warren/ Houston Chronicle)

Game 2
October 14, 2017 • Houston, Texas
Astros 2, Yankees 1

V IS FOR VERLANDER AND VICTORY

Ace's Complete Game Capped by Altuve's Mad Dash
By Brian T. Smith

Justin Verlander's baseball hero and childhood idol, Nolan Ryan, watched the endless beauty behind home plate. When Carlos Correa and Jose Altuve gathered before the Astros' eruption in the ninth inning, they told themselves they had to finish off the Yankees in Verlander's honor.

And even if A.J. Hinch had tried to remove the ball from his new ace's hands before the 124th pitch in Game 2 of the American League Championship Series, the manager knew exactly what Verlander would say.

Go away.

This is still my game to win.

I'm not leaving the mound.

"I would have had to rip the ball away from that man if I was going to take him out," said Hinch, after Correa ripped a game-winning double to right field. Altuve kept racing toward home, and the Astros celebrated a 2-0 lead in the ALCS by going crazy at Minute Maid Park in one of the most thrilling playoff finishes in franchise history.

The 2017 Astros aren't two wins away from the World Series without Verlander.

Heck, they might not be playing in the middle of October.

Verlander changed his life at the last minute just before August became September, suddenly agreeing to become a Houstonian. Since then, all the 34-year-old righthander has done is arrive at Minute Maid on the day the Astros started playing home games again after Hurricane Harvey, dominate the mound on the day his new team captured the AL West, shut down Boston in Game 1 of the AL Division Series, emerge out of the pen for the first time in his career to clinch Game 4, then silence New York 2-1 in Game 2 of the ALCS.

Verlander is a stunning 8-0 with 59 strikeouts and just eight earned runs in 51 2/3 innings as an Astro.

He's 1998 Randy Johnson but ultimately even better – the best regular-season club in franchise history didn't make it past the NLDS.

And all the phone calls, text messages, pros and cons, and monumental life decisions Aug. 31 now make so much sense.

Verlander has been exactly what the 2017 Astros needed and arrived at the absolutely perfect time. Saturday at Minute Maid was one of the strongest and most inspiring outings of his 13-year career, and the Astros aren't up 2-0 against New York without No. 35.

"When it came down to it, when I decided to say yes, these are the moments that you envision," said Verlander, who set a career playoff high with 13 strikeouts and limited the Yankees to five hits and one earned run in nine winning innings. "I was brought here to help this team

Justin Verlander walks off the field after ending the top of the eighth inning with three straight strikeouts during Game 2. Verlander was brilliant in the win, pitching a complete game with 13 strikeouts and only one earned run. (Karen Warren/Houston Chronicle)

win a championship. And I'm aware of that, and I'm going to do everything I possibly can.

"That's what it's all about, man. After that game is over and just kind of sitting in the clubhouse and having my teammates come over and say how much they appreciated that effort – that's what it's all about. That means everything to me."

In an era when starters are praised for just going seven, Verlander went the full, long, strong nine.

Ringing shouts and cheers in the eighth. Then the instant recognition of the rare and special during the final frame, with Minute Maid standing as one and proudly claiming Verlander as its own.

"That was probably the loudest I heard a ballpark or close to it. And I've been part of some pretty loud moments," said Verlander, who passed Johnson for the most 11-or-more strikeout playoff games in MLB history. "The way those fans were pushing me to finish that game – or finish the ninth inning and have a chance to win the game – I mean, that matters. It gets your adrenaline going."

So does this.

Verlander struck out the side in the eighth, and it was still 1-1. Then he returned to a roaring sea of orange in the ninth, endured a Didi Gregorius line-drive single to record three more outs, and the score didn't move.

So before Yankees fireballer Aroldis Chapman took over and extra innings became real life, Correa turned to his close friend and spoke the truth.

We've got to do this for the team, Correa told Altuve. We've got to come through right now.

For 2-0 in the ALCS and two wins away from the World Series.

Because the man who chose the Astros on Aug. 31 had given everything he had for the Astros in Game 2.

"(Altuve's) like, 'OK, let's do it,'" Correa said.

Altuve single.

Correa liner to right-center.

Third-base coach Gary Pettis windmilling Altuve toward home. The ball arriving early, then bouncing around. The Astros leaping and shouting and believing, making all 124 of Verlander's pitches count.

The ace delivered like an old-school horse, mirroring the idol watching him from the seats.

Jose Altuve celebrates after tagging home to score the winning run on Carlos Correa's walk off double in the ninth inning of Game 2. (Karen Warren/Houston Chronicle)

"Because of his success and the style of pitcher he is, I've watched his career since he came on the scene as a rookie," Ryan said in September.

The Astros followed Verlander's lead, never gave in, and finally forced the Yankees to.

"Big moments are meant for big-time performers. From pitch one, Justin Verlander was big for this team. Really, pitch one as an Astro," Hinch said. "But most importantly, this game (Saturday), he was exceptional in every way. From controlling his emotions to executing every pitch to being dominant with his fastball, the put-away breaking ball, a couple changeups.

"He just was every bit the top-end pitcher in the league that he's been for a really long time. This is such a big moment for our team. But he put us on his back with his pitching."

They wanted him for this time. He came here for this moment.

And in Game 2 of the ALCS, Verlander won it for the Astros. ■

Above: The Astros celebrate around shortstop Carlos Correa who hit the game-winning RBI double. (Michael Ciaglo/Houston Chronicle) Opposite: Jose Altuve hits a single during the ninth inning of the Game 2 win. The hit sparked the rally that would lead to a crucial victory. (Michael Ciaglo/Houston Chronicle)

Game 3
October 16, 2017 • New York City, New York
Yankees 8, Astros 1

APPLE JACKS

Frazier, Judge Hit 3-Run Homers to Put New York Back in Series
By Jake Kaplan

For as well as everything went for the Astros in the first two games of this American League Championship Series, with seemingly every bounce going their way, the third installment followed a script to disaster.

Charlie Morton succumbed to a pair of two-out rallies. Cameron Maybin cost his starting pitcher an out on a terribly misplayed fly ball. Evan Gattis failed to block a curveball in the dirt with a runner on third base.

And the New York Yankees' bats awoke to narrow a series that before Monday night at Yankee Stadium had been controlled by the Astros.

An 8-1 rout halved the Astros' series lead to 2-1 and ensured their stay in the Big Apple will last through Wednesday night. The Astros will rely on Lance McCullers Jr. to set the tone on the mound in Game 4. His performance could be moot if their bats don't get going. Through three games, their major league-leading offense has produced only five runs.

Veteran lefthander CC Sabathia and relievers Adam Warren held the Astros scoreless through eight innings of Game 3. A bases-loaded walk by Alex Bregman against Tommy Kahnle in the ninth accounted for the Astros' lone run. They left 11 runners on base. Even the mighty Jose Altuve was held hitless in four at-bats.

"It's frustrating over all," right fielder Josh Reddick said. "We've got to get the big hits when we need them."

Morton was charged with seven earned runs in a line that won't do his pitching justice. Two scored on a three-run homer by Aaron Judge that served as the Yankees' knockout blow. After running defensive clinics in Games 1 and 2, the Astros' gloves let them down in Game 3.

Maybin's misplay at the start of a five-run fourth inning for the Yankees loomed largest. It occurred on a fly ball down the left-field line off the bat of Greg Bird. The speedy Maybin, who was shifted toward center field, raced toward the ball in time to get under it but pulled up as he neared its landing spot. The ball took a high bounce into the stands for a leadoff ground-rule double.

Bird later scored when a Will Harris curveball in the dirt skirted past Gattis and to the backstop. Judge followed with his homer, which closed the book on Morton.

Morton displayed his usual filthy stuff, particularly early in his outing. In his first meeting with Judge, he reached back for 98 mph on his fastball and struck him out on an 89 mph cutter. He snapped off nasty curveballs to strike out Brett Gardner in the first and Bird in the second.

Morton's evening took a turn for the worse with two outs in the second inning. Starlin Castro reached on a dribbler Bregman failed to barehand. Aaron Hicks dunked a single into left-center field. And then Todd Frazier changed the game with surely one of the most unassuming home runs in postseason history.

On a 95 mph fastball Morton threw down and away, the right-handed hitting Frazier poked it the opposite way to right field. Off the bat, it looked like a pop fly. But

Jose Altuve scoops up a grounder by Yankees shortstop Didi Gregorius to force him out at first base during the fourth inning of Game 3. (Michael Ciaglo/Houston Chronicle)

as Reddick ran toward the wall, the ball continued to carry. It landed in the seats, with an estimated distance of 365 feet.

"If you were to show me a video of his swing, the pitch speed and the location, I would have never thought (home run)," said Morton, who added he actually intended to throw the fastball inside. "That was unbelievable. Just a great piece of hitting."

Morton worked around a one-out walk of Judge in a scoreless third before disaster struck in the fourth.

It started with Maybin

"I was thinking if I dove for it and missed it, it was probably going to be a triple," he said. "Of course you don't know it's going to bounce into the seats. But we talked about it. Just a play where you're down, I think you've just got to take a shot and whatever happens happens.

"But (it was) just a tough play. You've got to just give those guys credit. They did a good job of taking advantage."

After the Bird double, Morton induced a groundout from Castro and a fly out from Hicks on which Bird advanced to third. He then walked Frazier, who scored on a well-placed single by Chase Headley, the first hit of this postseason by a Yankees designated hitter in 29 at-bats. An errant curveball with which Morton hit Gardner loaded the bases for Judge.

The hit by pitch spelled the end for Morton, whom manager A.J. Hinch replaced with Harris. Harris, who hadn't pitched since Game 1 of the ALDS on Oct. 5, jumped ahead in the count with a cut fastball before mixing in his first curveball. Gattis failed to block it, and Bird trotted home to give the Yankees a five-run lead.

"It just got away from me," Gattis said. "That ball's got to be blocked."

Moments later, the Astros' deficit reached eight. On Harris' 2-and-2 pitch, an up-and-in fastball the pitcher called for, Judge sent it on a line over the fence in left field. The homer was Judge's second of the postseason but his first since the Yankees' Wild Card Game win over the Minnesota Twins on Oct. 3.

"That was the pitch I wanted to throw," Harris said. "I thought I had him set up for it, and I didn't. He was ready." ■

Yankees right fielder Aaron Judge hits a three-run home run off of Astros relief pitcher Will Harris during the fourth inning of Game 3. (Karen Warren/Houston Chronicle)

Game 4
October 17, 2017 • New York City, New York
Yankees 6, Astros 4

POISON PEN

Devenski, Musgrove, Giles Allow 5 Runs, Spoil McCullers' Gem
By Jake Kaplan

Another eighth inning. Another bullpen collapse. Another stellar Lance McCullers Jr. start wasted.

Two Octobers after their nightmarish Game 4 of the ALDS against the Kansas City Royals, the Astros saw their best relievers melt down yet again in a 6-4 defeat in Game 4 of the ALCS against the Yankees. The stunning loss turned a potential three-games-to-one lead into a 2-2 tie and ensured the best-of-seven series will return to Minute Maid Park for Game 6.

"The series wasn't over after two games," Astros manager A.J. Hinch said. "It's certainly not over after four."

Leading 4-2 after seven innings, the Astros were six outs shy of being a win away from clinching their franchise's second World Series appearance. A victory would have created the opportunity to close it out at Yankee Stadium with ace lefthander Dallas Keuchel on the mound.

Instead, they must win two of their next three. After starting Keuchel opposite Masahiro Tanaka in Game 5, they will pitch co-ace Justin Verlander in Game 6, likely opposite Luis Severino. A potential Game 7 would be played Saturday, also at Minute Maid Park.

In Game 4, McCullers gave the Astros as dominant a performance as they could have expected, especially considering he hadn't started since Sept. 30 and had started only three times since August. In his second career postseason start – his first came in the aforementioned Game 4 of the '15 ALDS – he held a dangerous Yankees lineup to one run in six-plus innings.

Their bullpen rested, the Astros appeared to be in great shape. But their three best relievers, Chris Devenski, Joe Musgrove and Ken Giles, combined to surrender five runs on six hits and two walks while recording just four outs.

"It's painful now," Giles said in the clubhouse after the game. "I let my team down."

Musgrove and Giles combined to allow the four runs in the Yankees' four-run eighth. Giles was on the mound for all four after inheriting two baserunners from Musgrove. The two biggest Yankees swings came from Aaron Judge, who tied the game with a double off the top of the left-field wall, and Gary Sanchez, who cracked a go-ahead two-run double to right-center field.

Aroldis Chapman closed things down in the top of the ninth for the Yankees. Despite their series-high four runs, the Astros' major league-best offense still has yet to show up. Through four games, they're batting a dismal .153 with six extra-base hits in 118 at-bats. They had 18 extra-base hits over their four ALDS games against Boston.

"We have to keep fighting," designated hitter Carlos Beltran said. "It wasn't going to be easy."

McCullers pitched the best he had since a June 8 start at Kansas City when he allowed only two hits in seven

Jose Altuve throws over New York Yankees first baseman Greg Bird as he turns a double play on a grounder by Starlin Castro in Game 4. (Michael Ciaglo/Houston Chronicle)

innings of one-run ball. The lone run he gave up Tuesday came on the final pitch he threw, a first-pitch power curveball that Judge blasted out to center field. McCullers allowed only two hits and two walks.

"It's the best I've felt in many, many months," he said. "I've been trying to tell anyone with ears that, but it seemed like it was not being heard all the time.

"I'm glad I got an opportunity to show the team that I feel good, and I'm ready to go moving forward."

The Astros led 4-0 midway through the sixth inning. Sonny Gray matched McCullers for the first five innings before Yankees manager Joe Girardi lifted him with runners on first and second base for Jose Altuve. After Altuve drew a walk against David Robertson, Yuli Gurriel delivered the game's biggest swing to that point with a three-run double down the left-field line.

Gurriel's double alone drove in the most runs the Astros have scored in any of the four games of this series. Marwin Gonzalez doubled off Chad Green in the seventh and scored on the second of two fielding errors committed by second baseman Starlin Castro.

After Judge's homer spelled the end of McCullers' night, Devenski narrowed the score further by allowing a triple to Didi Gregorius and a sacrifice fly to Sanchez. A walk of Greg Bird ensured his exit, and Musgrove was called on to escape the inning.

Hinch sent Musgrove back out for the eighth, and the righthander promptly allowed consecutive singles to Todd Frazier and pinch hitter Chase Headley. On his hit to the left-center field gap, Headley stumbled between first and second base. The relay throw from the outfield came in to shortstop Carlos Correa, who adhered to the instructions of a teammate yelling "one, one" and fired to first base.

Headley continued on toward second base. Gurriel received Correa's throw and fired back to Altuve at second in time to get Headley. But Altuve was late to make the tag.

"I think (Gurriel) made a really good throw," Altuve said. "But you know, I'm 5-5. Headley was like 6-something. So he kind of like blocked me, and I decided to take a step back to make sure I catch that ball. If I don't do it, I don't think I would've caught that ball."

The sequence spelled the end of Musgrove's night. Hinch tabbed Giles to face the top of the Yankees' order. Brett Gardner plated Frazier from third base on a groundout to Altuve before Judge unloaded on a Giles slider for his double.

A Gregorius single put runners on the corners for Sanchez, who capitalized on a mistake pitch by Giles. In a 2-and-0 count, the Astros closer intended to pitch inside to Sanchez. Instead, he left a 98 mph fastball over the plate.

"We just couldn't get the inning to end," Hinch said. "We were trying to match up and get and make pitches. They were putting really great at-bats together. Even their outs, they had productive outs. Nobody likes that term, but they got 90 feet whenever they needed to, whether it was the sac fly or Gardner's ground ball to second base.

"The key really in that inning is not turning Headley's ball into an out. We had an out – obviously, Carlos was making an athletic play, Yuli makes an athletic play, Jose tries to tag him, it goes to replay, and we don't get the out. Looking back, I think that was a big play because it set up a ton of pressure on us for the rest of the inning with guys all over the place." ■

Lance McCullers Jr. pitches to Yankees catcher Gary Sanchez during the fourth inning of Game 4. McCullers pitched six strong innings, giving up only one earned run. (Karen Warren/Houston Chronicle)

Game 5
October 18, 2017 • New York City, New York
Yankees 5, Astros 0

ALL IS AMISS

Keuchel Gets No Backing as Team Batting Average Falls to .147 for Series
By Jake Kaplan

If the Astros fail to win the two consecutive games they require to advance to the World Series, their American League Championship Series against the New York Yankees will be remembered for the mystifying disappearing act of their major league-best offense.

Their offensive struggles in the ALCS reached a nadir in a 5-0 loss in Game 5 at Yankee Stadium. Shut out for the first time in the playoffs since the final game of the 2005 World Series, they managed only four hits a day after mustering just three.

A third straight defeat in the Bronx left them headed home on the brink of elimination. The Yankees lead the best-of-seven series three games to two. Game 6 is Friday at Minute Maid Park. The Astros will start their best pitcher in Justin Verlander. His performance will go only so far if their bats can't hit the Yankees' best, Luis Severino.

Yankees starter Masahiro Tanaka shut down the Astros for the first seven innings of Game 5 before handing the baton to reliever Tommy Kahnle. The Astros were 0-for-8 with runners in scoring position, dropping their series total to 4-for-27.

The offense's regression from the regular season has been staggering. A group that produced 5.5 runs per game has scored only nine times in five ALCS games. The Astros batted an incredible .282 with a .346 on-base percentage and .478 slugging percentage in the regular season. They are slashing a putrid .147/.234/.213 in this series.

Carlos Correa's solo home run in Game 2 at Minute Maid Park signifies the Astros' only long ball of this series. They hit 1.47 homers per game in the regular season.

A sampling of the individual numbers looks just as ugly.
- Josh Reddick is 0-for-17.
- George Springer is 2-for-18.
- Alex Bregman is 2-for-17.
- Marwin Gonzalez is 2-for-15.
- Carlos Beltran is 1-for-12.
- Brian McCann is 0-for-10.
- Collectively, the Astros have a mere 22 hits in 150 at-bats.

"From what I see, it seems like we're trying to do way too much in the box," said Reddick, who in the regular season never went more than two consecutive games without a hit. "Everybody's trying to be the one guy who can put the team on their back with one swing, and I think that's one thing that we can't really get too focused on.

"We've got to keep the line moving. We've been so great all year chaining together hits one after another. We've just got to get back to that."

The anemic Astros offense left ace lefthander Dallas Keuchel little margin for error Wednesday. And for the first time in nine career starts against these Yankees, he was knocked around some.

Keuchel, who had allowed seven earned runs in his 57 2/3 previous innings against the Yankees, allowed four

Brad Peacock walks back to the mound as Yankees catcher Gary Sanchez rounds the bases after hitting a solo home run during the seventh inning of Game 5. (Michael Ciaglo/Houston Chronicle)

in only 4 2/3 frames Wednesday. The Yankees tagged him with seven hits, including two doubles. Three singles in a five-batter span in the fifth chased Keuchel from the game.

The outing inflated Keuchel's career ERA against the Yankees a half-run, from his incredible 1.09 to 1.59. He had allowed more than two earned runs in a start against them only once before, on Aug. 21, 2014, when he gave up just three in eight innings.

"I knew I had my hands full today with the way their starters have been throwing against us," he said. "But at the same time, I thought coming into it we had a great game plan and with the pitches we've been throwing and strategy and the counts that it was going to be another pitchers' duel. It just didn't go our way, and we'll look to regroup and get back to Houston."

The second inning contrasted the states of these two offenses. In the top of the frame, the Astros squandered a leadoff double by Yuli Gurriel. In the bottom, the Yankees capitalized on a two-out double by Starlin Castro when Greg Bird ripped a single to the right-field corner.

Gonzalez provided another prime scoring opportunity for the Astros in the fifth. After ripping a single to right field off Tanaka, he advanced to second on a wild pitch. McCann worked a walk to bring up the top of the order, which during most of the regular season would have meant doom for the pitcher.

But Springer and Reddick both struck out against Tanaka. Springer was caught looking at a fastball at the knees on the outside corner. Reddick chased a splitter outside.

Tanaka struck out eight and issued only one walk in his seven innings. The Astros, according to Hinch, got "pull happy" against the Japanese righthander. He induced 10 outs on the ground and four in the air.

"He was pitching on the edges. That's what he does. That's his MO," Bregman said. "He's going to throw fastballs on the edges to both sides of the plate. He's going to throw splitters down in the zone, and his slider was good tonight. It was on the edges.

"He's a good pitcher, and we didn't capitalize when we needed to. We just need one big swing – one big swing to get us going – and the offense will be back."

Keuchel struck out eight in his 4 2/3 innings and walked only one, but his outing was doomed by the Yankees' two-run fifth.

Chase Headley began the Yanks' biggest rally with a one-out single on which he reached second after Bregman's throw skipped past Gurriel. A groundout by Brett Gardner brought Keuchel one out from escaping unscathed.

With Judge due up next, Hinch jogged out to the mound, and the infield convened around Keuchel. The meeting was brief. Keuchel pitched to Judge, but carefully. A walk set the stage for Gary Sanchez, one of the Yankees' Game 4 heroes.

Sanchez ripped a single down the left-field line that scored Headley. Didi Gregorius ran his count full before singling up the middle just past diving second baseman Jose Altuve. The three consecutive New York baserunners prompted the end of Keuchel's outing. As he walked toward the dugout, the Yankees fans sitting behind the Astros' dugout waved him goodbye.

In the visitors' clubhouse after the game, before the Astros packed their bags and boarded a flight for Houston, veterans Beltran and McCann led a team meeting.

"The message was that we cannot feel sorry about ourselves. We won the first two games, we lost the three games here, and now we're going to have the opportunity to go home and try to do what they did here," Beltran said. "Win the next two games and try to move on to the next round. That's the mentality.

"I told them that it wasn't going to be easy. Even though you win the first two games, we have to understand that we're coming here to their home. They've been able to play good games here, so that's what they did. ... You have to give them credit, but at the end of the day, we have to be able to as a team turn the page and move on and look to what is ahead of us." ■

Astros starting pitcher Dallas Keuchel reacts as Yankees left fielder Brett Gardner hits a grounder to first, with Chase Headley getting forced out at second during the third inning of Game 5. Keuchel had a rare poor outing against the Yankees, giving up four earned runs in 4 2/3 innings. (Michael Ciaglo/Houston Chronicle)

Game 6
October 20, 2017 • Houston, Texas
Astros 7, Yankees 1

AN ACE IN PLACE

Verlander Continues Remarkable Run, Forces Game 7

By Brian T. Smith

They wanted and needed him, so he finally joined them.

Aug. 31: the day that forever changed the 2017 Astros.

When they won the American League West, Justin Verlander owned the mound and then joyously ran around the field.

When they handed him the ball out of the bullpen for the first time in his career during Game 4 of the American League Division Series, he held off the Red Sox in the Fenway Park rain, then his new team clinched and sprayed champagne.

And in the biggest, most critical game of this thrilling season – the wild-card Yankees one win away from the World Series; the 101-win Astros holding on, trying to survive for one more day – Verlander was playoff perfection once again.

It's ridiculous, really. Hollywood and storybook-like.

Being so untouchable on a national stage, over and over again, when he's brand new in orange and blue.

In the AL Championship Series: 16 innings, 21 strikeouts, one measly earned run.

In elimination-game playoff starts: 4-1 with 41 K's and a 1.21 ERA.

With the team that wanted and needed him, and is just one win away from the World Series because of him: a perfect 9-0 with 67 strikeouts and a surreal 1.23 ERA.

Verlander has two of the Astros' three victories in the ALCS and four playoff wins in 2017.

If his new club captures Game 7 against New York on Saturday night back at Minute Maid Park, the 34-year-old righthander who has absolutely owned October will soon be facing the Los Angeles Dodgers in the World Series.

"He's been everything that we could have hoped for and more," said manager A.J. Hinch, after the Astros took Game 6 7-1 on Friday behind seven more scoreless innings from Verlander and tied the series 3-3. "This guy prepares.

"He rises to the moment. He's incredibly focused and locked in during games, and emptied his tank (Friday)."

George Springer leapt toward the roof near the 404-foot mark in center field at the perfect time.

Brian McCann broke through.

Jose Altuve went 2-for-4 with three RBIs and clubbed his fourth home run of the postseason.

Carlos Correa and Yuli Gurriel answered Aaron Judge's solo shot in the eighth inning with back-to-back hits as the Astros' bats finally woke up and cracked wood for the first time in this series.

"I believe in my team. (Saturday) is going to be a good night," Altuve said.

But just as in Game 2 of the ALCS – 124 pitches, nine old-school innings, 13 K's – Hinch's club doesn't capture win-or-end Game 6 and move one step closer toward the Fall Classic without No. 35.

Yankees moment?

Try Astros history. And MLB: Verlander is the first

Justin Verlander continued his remarkable postseason with seven dominant innings, giving up no runs and striking out eight. (Karen Warren/Houston Chronicle)

pitcher in baseball history with three consecutive scoreless starts in elimination games and hasn't allowed a run in 24 straight innings during elimination starts.

"There's no point in saving anything. … It's just kind of I'm out there until I'm not out there any longer," Verlander said. "In season, you sometimes have, OK, you get deep in the game here, let me try to save some pitches.

"In a playoff, that's out the window, specifically in a 0-0 ballgame in a decisive game."

Verlander's run is among the greatest and most important for the Astros since major league baseball arrived in this city in 1962.

All the trade rumors and prospects-for-an-October-ace questions that surrounded the Astros for weeks – months, really – during the will-they-or-won't-they buildup toward Aug. 31?

Perfect hindsight now.

"He's one of the greatest pitchers of our generation," said Charlie Morton, who'll take the mound for the Astros in the ALCS finale.

Verlander was what they needed, willingly changing cities and colors minutes away from the deadline.

An artist, a stopper, a powerhouse throwback (and a reliever) who has thrown the Astros into a Game 7 for just the second time in franchise history.

"He was cruising early," Hinch said. "And then the last couple innings, it looked like he was spending a lot of energy out there. … Those last pitches were pretty high-stress.

"That was an incredible play by George in center field. And for Verlander to come back and get the last out, it just felt like that was enough."

Just five hits and one walk. Ninety-nine pitches for 70 strikes.

The arm, presence and experience to build a bridge to Game 7, with Verlander gradually losing track of the innings and batters and focusing only on the next necessary pitch.

In a season defined by record-setting home runs and 100-win teams, Verlander has the Astros in sight of the World Series by owning the mound.

"He's pitched great, and you have to give him a lot of credit," said New York's CC Sabathia, who'll start the final game of the ALCS.

Game 2 against New York felt like the peak point for Verlander. His mentor and childhood idol Nolan Ryan watched up close. Hinch then joked after nine shutdown innings that he'd have to rip the ball out of his starter's hands to remove him from the game.

Friday, Verlander gave and gave again.

For the team that wanted and needed him.

For the 43,179 so proud to now have him in orange and blue.

For the 2017 Astros and the Game 7 that can send them all the way to the World Series.

"It's pretty amazing to me how quickly these fans have bonded to me and vice versa," Verlander said. "I feel it, I appreciate it, especially on the field. But around town, everybody is just wishing good luck. … People, a lot of times in new cities, if they're not baseball fans, they might not recognize me. But it seems like a lot of people here, they're involved, and they want this team to win.

"And they always come up and give me their blessing and want me to know they care, and that means a lot."

Nine Astros victories for the new ace, four in the playoffs.

Doing what he was brought here to do each time and resetting the bar higher and higher with each instantly memorable postseason start.

These Astros are hosting a Game 7.

They're alive in 2017 because of Verlander. ∎

Astros first baseman Yuli Gurriel slides home after an Alex Bregman two-run double in the eighth inning of Game 6. The offense finally came alive, pounding the Yankees for seven runs. (Karen Warren/Houston Chronicle)

Game 7
October 21, 2017 • Houston, Texas
Astros 4, Yankees 0

REACHING FOR THE STARS

Brilliance of Morton, McCullers Secures Pennant, Second World Series Trip for Franchise

By Jake Kaplan

As he tracked the ball through the air, Jose Altuve clung to his bat with his right hand. He ran almost the entire way down the first-base line this way until he was sure he had hit a home run, at which point he flipped his bat near the coach's box.

The heroes were many in the 4-0 victory over the New York Yankees that punched the Astros' ticket to only their second World Series in 56 seasons Saturday night at a raucous Minute Maid Park. Charlie Morton recorded the first 15 outs, Lance McCullers Jr. the last 12. Brian McCann came through in the clutch. Alex Bregman cut down a run with his arm.

But it was fitting Altuve provided the most majestic moment of Game 7 of the American League Championship Series. Perhaps soon to be the league's Most Valuable Player, the 5-foot-6 second baseman is the heart and soul of the Astros. He was their best player and their constant on the field through their drastic tear-down and long-term rebuild and now for their return to prominence.

On Tuesday night, Altuve will lead his team onto the field at Dodger Stadium for Game 1 of the World Series. His Astros clinched their appearance in the Fall Classic by holding home field in each of their four ALCS games at Minute Maid Park, where they were backed by the most boisterous crowds of the season.

"It means a lot because, obviously, we've been working really hard for this," Altuve said. "I know a lot of people see the Houston Astros going to the World Series, but they don't see all the effort that we put in for a lot of years to become American League champions. This is awesome. I'm really excited and proud about every single guy on my team."

Saturday night's win served as validation for the Astros' dark years from 2011 to 2014. It also lifted up a city that will long be recovering from the devastation of Hurricane Harvey. Since its inception, this franchise has advanced to the World Series only once before, in 2005, when it lost to the Chicago White Sox. The Astros have never won a World Series game.

They will have at least four opportunities beginning this week. They claimed the club's first Game 7 victory behind dominant pitching and highlight-reel worthy defense. Their offense accumulated a series-high 10 hits.

Morton and McCullers held the Yankees to only three.

"We had to make a decision on which guy was going to start, which guy was going to relieve," Astros manager A.J. Hinch said. "We knew we were going to use both of them. I didn't know they were going to split the game and get us all 27 outs."

Morton set the tone with five scoreless innings on just 54 pitches. The 33-year-old righthander has pitched in the majors since 2008 but until this year, his first with the Astros, had been plagued by injury after injury. The Astros took a risk by signing him in the offseason to a two-year

The Astros celebrate their 4-0 win over the Yankees in Game 7, rallying from a 3-2 series deficit and claiming each of the last two games at Minute Maid Park. (Brett Coomer/Houston Chronicle)

deal worth up to $19 million after incentives. He repaid them and then some.

"That crowd was unbelievable to have at my back," Morton said, goggles atop his head amid yet another champagne celebration. "It got me fired up more than any crowd I've ever pitched in front of."

McCann, who caught Morton in his major league debut with Atlanta nine Junes ago, was another of the Astros' key offseason acquisitions. They acquired him in a November trade from these same Yankees, who have a budding star at catcher in Gary Sanchez. To obtain better prospects in the deal, New York agreed to pay $5.5 million of McCann's annual $17 million salary.

McCann helped to beat his former team Saturday. For the second consecutive night, his double to the right-field corner proved to be one of the most important hits of the game. This one, off Tommy Kahnle in a three-run fifth inning, gave the Astros a 4-0 lead.

The margin allowed Hinch to leverage McCullers, who started Game 3 of the series, for a four-inning save. The 24-year-old righthander struck out six and allowed only one hit. Forty one of his 54 pitches, including his final 24, were power curveballs.

"The second half (of the season), I struggled real bad. When I finally got healthy again and I knew I was healthy, I told myself, 'Hey, when you come out here, it's time to put some respect back on your name,' " McCullers said.

"I wanted to prove that I'm always going to be the pitcher that people know I can be when I'm able to be that guy. I just wanted to show my teammates that, 'Yes, I was absent for the second half, but I have your back now.' "

The Astros scored three runs off Kahnle in a game-changing fifth. Before McCann broke open the game with his double, Altuve also punished a changeup for his fifth home run of the playoffs. Though Altuve insisted his bat flip wasn't meant as disrespect, several of his teammates described it as payback for Kahnle's showing up Altuve

earlier in the series by screaming, "What, what, what," after striking him out earlier in the series.

When Altuve's line drive cleared the right-field fence Saturday, some in the Astros' dugout began to yell, "What, what, what," toward the mound.

"The bat flip," Altuve said, "was for my team."

Altuve's five postseason homers are the second most for an Astros player in a single postseason, trailing only Carlos Beltran's eight in 2004.

"He is the Houston Astro right now," Hinch said of Altuve. "The way he's played, what he's persevered through, the teams he's been on, and yet he's still hungry. He's not going to be satisfied with this celebration. He's not going to be satisfied with that home run. And that's what I love about him."

The Yankees had action in their bullpen as early as the bottom of the third inning. Their starter, veteran lefthander CC Sabathia, was nowhere near as sharp as he had been in his dominant Game 3 win at Yankee Stadium.

Still, Sabathia maneuvered his way in and out of trouble his first time and a half through the Astros' lineup. The Astros squandered a leadoff single by George Springer in the first inning and could only watch as Yankees right fielder Aaron Judge robbed Yuli Gurriel of extra bases in the second.

In the fourth, the Astros struck. Leading off the inning, Evan Gattis fouled off three consecutive two-strike cutters before getting a pitch on which he could do damage. When Sabathia hung a slider, Gattis clobbered it out to left-center field for a solo shot that opened the scoring.

Before inning's end, Sabathia's evening was over. McCann drew a walk, and Josh Reddick snapped his 0-for-22 in the series with a shift-beating single into left field. Yankees manager Joe Girardi called on Kahnle to put out the fire. On Kahnle's first pitch, Springer grounded into an inning-ending double play.

Morton sailed through the first four innings, needing

Justin Verlander holds his MVP trophy while celebrating the Astros 4-0 win over the Yankees in Game 7. The late-season acquisition was instrumental in clinching the second World Series appearance in franchise history. (Brett Coomer/Houston Chronicle)

only 36 pitches (including 28 strikes) to record the first 12 outs. The first sign of trouble came in the fifth, which Greg Bird led off by ripping a double to the right-field corner.

Bird advanced to third base on a fourth-ball wild pitch by Morton to Aaron Hicks with one out, setting the stage for Todd Frazier, who homered off Morton in Game 3. In a 1-and-1 count, Morton threw a 95 mph down in the strike zone that Frazier mishit. The ball rolled to Bregman, who fired a perfect throw home to McCann, able to catch the ball and tag Bird in one motion.

"We had a play earlier in the year, about 10 games before the end of the regular season, and I tried to turn a double play, and the run scored," Bregman said. "So before the pitch, I was already ready where if it was hit softly, I was going to throw the guy out at the plate, and if it was hit hard, I was going to turn the double play.

"As soon as it was hit, I thought, 'Hey, you better put this on the cash,' and I pulled out the inner Peyton Manning and threw a dime."

Bregman's throw changed the complexion of the inning. With runners on first and second and two outs, Morton induced a groundout from Chase Headley to escape the jam. Hinch called on McCullers to face the top of the Yankees' order at the start of the sixth.

McCullers gave Hinch 12 pivotal outs in relief. Springer sealed one of them with another spectacular leaping catch in center field to steal extra bases from Bird in the seventh. Hinch got Will Harris up in the eighth after McCullers issued a walk to Frazier to begin the inning. McCullers responded by retiring the next three batters, punctuating the frame by striking out Judge on three straight curveballs.

Ken Giles warmed in the top of the ninth, but the inning belonged to McCullers. He struck out Didi Gregorius and Sanchez before inducing a pop out to shallow center field from Bird. As soon as Bird made contact, McCullers threw his arms up in the air.

The Astros had won the pennant.

"This is a special feeling. I can't even describe it," shortstop Carlos Correa said. "I got drafted in 2012, and now in 2017 I'm going to the World Series. I don't think it gets any better than that."

"You dream about this as a little kid," Bregman said. "We're living a dream." ■

Lance McCullers Jr. reacts to striking out Yankees right fielder Aaron Judge to end the top of the eighth inning of Game 7. McCullers pitched four strong innings out of the bullpen, earning the save in the series clinching win. (Karen Warren/Houston Chronicle)

Jose Altuve kisses his daug[...]
while celebrating the Astros[...]
win over the Yankees in Gar[...]
Altuve hit his fifth homer o[...]
postseason in the game, contin[...]
his dominant 2017 season. (K[...]
Warren/Houston Chror[...]